FEMALES AND YOUNGER MEN

FAYM

Judith Brower Fancher

the Peppertree Press

Sarasota, Florida

DEDICATION

This book is dedicated to my grandmother, Eve, who lived up to her name as a "first" woman in every way; to my father Martin Brower, who is the greatest writer I know; to my mother, Tamar Brower, who brilliantly edited my book and made it work; and to my husband Charles E. Fancher, Jr., who came along like a white knight and took me with him to live happily ever after.

TABLE OF CONTENTS

CHAPTER 1

Doubling Your Chances at Love

Over the course of this book, you'll learn that the reasons why women haven't considered dating younger men in the past are either no longer relevant in today's society or were never relevant in the first place. From doubts about men's maturity, to mating and family planning anxieties, to economic influences, to growing old together, there are no sound arguments against choosing a younger man.

In fact, in quite a few instances, FAYM (Female And Younger Male) relationships can turn out to be wonderfully compatible—perhaps even more so than traditional pairings. This can be true for young women, women in their seventies, single women, divorced women, and widowed women. Hundreds of thousands of women all over the world—and particularly in the United States—have already realized that this is spot on and have embarked on exciting, loving, and lasting relationships with men who happen to be a few years younger than they are.

The first place you can see this happening is, of course, Hollywood, America's cultural proving ground. When Cher first dipped her toes into the pool of younger men in the 1980s, many women thought, "Sure, it works for Cher, but she's *Cher*. It would never work for me." But then, over time, Susan Sarandon, Madonna, and now, Demi Moore followed suit. As more female celebrities chose younger men, the FAYM relationship first gained public attention and then, more slowly, public approval.

We've now graduated from a Hollywood that produced *The Graduate*—in which a relationship between a woman and a younger man is portrayed as twisted and disgusting—to a Hollywood that produces movies like *Something's Gotta Give* and television series like *Sex and The City*, where we see examples of females and younger males in healthy, loving relationships.

On the big screen and on the red carpet, from Tinsel town to your hometown, FAYM relationships have not only become commonplace, but they're something to celebrate and romanticize. Why shouldn't they be? In so many ways that I'll mention over the course of this book, the FAYM relationship is simply more in sync than the traditional man-and-younger-woman pairing.

If the man is younger, a man and woman will be at their sexual peaks for a longer overlapping period. They'll also, to put it bluntly, both be *alive* for a longer intersecting period of time, if we use average life expectancies as a gauge.

Psychologically, the younger a man is, the more likely he'll be to subscribe fully to a culture of gender equality and, therefore, to see women as they see themselves. He'll also be less likely to bring all kinds of psychological and literal baggage into the relationship—from mental hang ups to prying ex-spouses.

But avoiding the baggage that comes with more years doesn't mean sacrificing maturity. As we'll see, maturity is not automatically tied to a person's age, and so a discerning woman can just as easily find a mature prospect among younger men as among older men.

Finally, she'll get to discover for the first time—as men have for centuries—the joys of sharing her guidance, connections, and comparative wealth with an appreciative younger partner.

It's a pretty rosy picture, right? So what's keeping many women from testing the waters? Even as thousands of American women discover the limitless potential of dating younger men, many women still shy away from the idea. Given how strongly our culture has reacted against it, it's in some ways understandable.

No one wants to be associated with that mean-spirited caricature, the "cougar" on the prowl. She's sexually voracious, yet totally undesirable. Her partners are manipulated, coerced, or preyed upon rather than willing and mutual participants. But here's the good news: That stereotype rose out of ignorance and fear, and it's disappearing quickly.

The same phenomenon happened a generation ago with interracial marriage. With each new generation, interracial marriage gets more and more blasé. The more it happens—the more people see their neighbors, friends, and family members engaging in it without the sky falling or any adverse consequences whatsoever—the more people realize, "Hey, no big deal."

Look around you. You'll see the exact same thing happening with FAYM relationships. It's hard to imagine that a 38 year-old woman and a 35 year-old man aren't equals, and people are starting to wise up. You might even be able to point to several couples that you personally know where the man is a few years younger than the woman is. Perhaps, you really didn't give it a second thought. You might not have even realized it before because, most of the time, you can't see the age difference just by looking. I guarantee that the couple doesn't notice the age difference in their interactions any more than the outside world notices it from their appearances. It's just a non-issue.

Women and men have simply begun to realize that there is no point in asking, "How old are you?" before going on a date. In fact, the trend is gaining such momentum that in a few years, it will seem completely absurd that a stigma ever existed. This book will seem like a relic—just like the ridiculous 1950s manners books telling women to be sure to remove their aprons before their husbands come home from work.

So, if you happen to be one of the women who just hasn't thought about dating younger men before, it's my hope that this book will be a step forward in your search for love. It's perfectly natural if the young-er-man option didn't occur to you; after all, our society has done a pretty darn good job of marginalizing FAYM relationships but not in any lasting way.

It's just too obvious and too simple: FAYM relationships work, and there's absolutely no foundation for the stigma against them. Once you realize this, your horizon expands immeasurably. All this time, you've had options for finding love among men your age and about ten years older. Now, you can literally increase your dating pool by 100 percent.

Suddenly, you have all these wonderful options among men as many as ten years younger than you are. You have 100 percent more opportunity to find a man you love and to start a wonderful life together. Likely, you'll realize younger men have even more going for them than you might have imagined—perhaps, even more than the older guys you've been dating in the past.

Here's the really beautiful thing. This doesn't just increase women's chances of finding love—it increases men's chances, too.

All the things pointed out over the course of this book that make FAYM relationships a great option are true for *both partners* in the relationship. Men will be just as excited to discover this option as women will be. But, just like women, they might not have thought of it previously. So, help a male friend or your brother, cousin, or nephew by sharing this idea with them.

They might be missing the love they've been seeking for the last ten years, which could be remedied by this simplest, most obvious solution.

Maybe the sixth grader they had a crush on when they were in fourth grade is still single. Maybe your 25 year-old male friend just didn't think about the fact that it's okay for him to ask out the now 27 year old woman! Or maybe your 65 year-old male friend can call her, even though she's 67 years old, and they can begin a wonderful relationship.

Share this new discovery with your girlfriends, certainly, but clue the guys in on it, too. You'll be giving all of them, men and women alike, the opportunity to expand by 100 percent their chances of finding love. Of course, you can give it a shot yourself. There's never been a better time to meet men, younger or older.

It used to be that people married right out of high school or college. They had a fairly limited age span of people to meet. Today, more and more people find their dates online, where the pool is always growing. But, if you're blinded by the old stigma, the online community can be just as limited.

Do you know that little search option that allows you to put in an age range for your potential dates? Many women are still stuck entering their own age—plus five or ten years older. See what happens if you expand your age group. Who knows, there may be quite a few younger men who would have been interested in you but never had the opportunity to see your profile because of your age filter.

Or if you're used to meeting men through your friends, go ahead and let your friends know that it would be okay for them to set you up with someone a few years younger. Maybe they know someone great for you, but they hesitated to suggest him because he was born after you. Or maybe they never thought of him themselves, and your little reminder will wake them up to thinking about personality and not birth dates. Suddenly, they'll realize, "Of course! She should meet Dan! I can't believe I never thought of it before."

Finally, the most important thing to remember when meeting men of any age is to keep an open mind. Have you ever heard anyone say, "Hi, nice to meet you! How old are you?" Of course not! It just doesn't happen.

So at parties, at work, at the bank—anywhere—there are always opportunities to meet people; keep your eyes peeled—for older *and* younger men. You'll have one eye pointing in each direction. It may make you look a little funny, but you just might find the person you're looking for.

When you do meet someone, don't let numbers make the decision for you. If you see someone attractive with a warm smile, and you think, "I'd like to get to know him," you're right. Give him a chance.

Go out with that younger guy and see if anybody out there blinks. See if *you* blink. See if you feel FAYMous! In short, there's nothing wrong—and everything right—about loving the younger man.

PART I:

THE TREND OF FEMALES AND YOUNGER MEN

CHAPTER 2

The New Look of Love

"Cindy, your 2 PM appointment Dale is here," the receptionist said. "And," the receptionist whispered, "he's gorgeous!"

Cindy, a single 32 year-old advertising executive, whose mind had previously been on her work, giggled in response. Then she double-checked her hair and lipstick—just in case the receptionist was right.

As Cindy came around the corner, a darling,

tow-headed, 20-something blonde with a Southern accent said, "Hi there!" And (if she didn't imagine it) he winked!

At the end of Cindy and Dale's meeting regarding direct mail, Dale invited her to think about coming to Thursday's Advertising Club mixer at a local restaurant. He even called her the next day to remind her about it. So, she agreed to go.

Thursday evening, at the end of the mixer, a very happily surprised Cindy was walked to her parking spot by the (she found out) 27 year-old Dale, who lingered by her car for a long time before reluctantly saying goodnight.

As she climbed in her car to drive home, Cindy thought about Dale. He was gorgeous, in her industry, single, and obviously going places in his career. It had also been obvious during the evening, once Cindy had arrived at the mixer, Dale had visibly broken into a delighted grin and spent the rest of the evening focused on her.

She realized that he definitely was very attracted to her. She also realized that she had purposely failed to mention her age when he told her how old he was, or rather how young he was. He was only 27, and Cindy was 32. "Obviously, it can't lead anywhere," she thought. And yet, he really was gorgeous and fun to talk with… She hated to pass up the opportunity.

* * *

For most people, nothing is more important than finding the right partner: a 24/7 friend, an anchor, a teammate, a true love, and a companion for life.

So what could be more wonderful than women discovering that they now have 100 percent more opportunity to find their soul mates?

This book uncovers a trend currently taking place that actually doubles the number of available males from which each woman can potentially find her match. The book also shows why this trend, which is so important to both genders, has only now begun to flourish.

There can be no doubt that during our lives, we witnessed an extraordinary social change in the United States, especially when it comes to that age-old question of love and marriage.

Go into any restaurant on a Saturday night, and you'll likely see every possible version of the concept of a "couple." There are couples with one Catholic and one Protestant, preppy people with tattooed people, older men with younger women, same-sex couples, couples with one Hispanic person and one Irish person, and couples with one person from the Eastside and one from the Southside.

These examples of formerly "taboo" love, love that only a few decades ago had to be concealed or just plain denied, are everywhere today—out in the open.

Beyond simply being visible, they've become commonplace. Largely, we don't look twice at couples that might have astonished our grandparents; their love is simply no longer cause for shock or even nosiness. It's no longer unusual. In this context, it might be tempting to think that society's bad habit of limiting who we can love and be loved by is a thing of the past.

Sidney Poitier's character in the 1967 film *Guess Who's Coming to Dinner* predicted that most stigmas—particularly those regarding interracial couples—would pass into history. For the most part, they have and rightly so. No reason exists why two human beings of different races, for example, can't date, fall in love, or marry. Overcoming a particular stigma was simply a matter of overcoming unreasonable and unfounded social prejudices.

In recent years, however, one last, tenacious stigma has slowly begun to fade away. The stigma has been so long-standing and engrained in our culture that we are overwhelmingly unconscious of it. I'm referring to the stigma against women dating younger men.

Chances are many people have never even thought about this issue. It's simply been taken for granted for so long in our society that women will date and marry men who are their own age or slightly older that we hardly pause to consider *why* we've set that restriction. It has remained somehow "weird" in our eyes to see a woman with a younger man. When we do see these couples, they become the butt of endless jokes.

But here's the trend: Society is changing, and women are indeed dating and marrying younger men.

Personally, I started to become aware of this trend when I realized that at least half of my single friends were dating or had dated slightly younger men. As I began to think about it, I realized that my own grandmother married a man eight years her junior. At the time, this was highly unusual. However, in the years following my grandmother's wedding (well over eighty years ago), increasing numbers of women followed suit.

We're not talking about the odd couple here and there; it's actually *a lot* of couples—hundreds of thousands of them. The more I noticed, the more I began to research, and I discovered that we are in fact in the middle of a full-scale global trend. The pattern is so overwhelming that I coined a term for this emerging kind of couple: the FAYM relationship, which stands for Females And Younger Men.

This book will focus on the United States, but the trend of FAYM relationships is certainly not limited to our country. One survey indicated that in Turkey in 1987, about 55,000 women married men younger than themselves. By 2006, that number had nearly doubled to 90,000. What is even more surprising about the doubling of the number of women marrying younger men in just two decades is that Turkey has been a society that continues to define marriage and life in a very traditional, conservative way.

The trend is even more apparent in the more progressive cultures of Western Europe. According to the BBC, for example, 15 percent of British brides were older than their grooms in 1963. Thirty-five years later, in 1998, that figure had risen to 26 percent or more than 1 in 4 marriages.

In the United States, the numbers are just as clear. On a Sunday in July 2009, for example, 7 of the 25 total wedding announcements in the venerable *New York Times* were for FAYM marriages. That's nearly 30 percent. The important thing to note is that this isn't a trend visible only in marriage statistics. It also applies to couples dating for fun and companionship who may not have their sights set on marriage.

The American Association of Retired Persons (AARP) recently reported that about 40 percent of Americans aged 45 and older are single due to divorce or the death of their spouse. That's millions of people. AARP was curious to know how these people are re-approaching the dating scene after the end of a first (or second, third, or fourth) marriage, so they conducted a survey of several thousand singles aged 40 to 69. They found that 34 percent of women in this age group—more than one-third!—date younger men.

It's clear that we're witnessing a global trend. Yet there is so much evidence, both first-hand and on the record, that this remains a stigmatized practice. For example, the publishers of the Turkish study cite a sociologist who claims that the FAYM trend is unhealthy and that it takes its cue from "a degeneration of the government system and a weakening of the family unit." The sociologist provides no statistics or research. One has to wonder if any supporting statistics even exist, or if this sociologist simply allowed his preconception of long-held beliefs get the best of him.

This same discomfort is present in the United States as well. My female friends who date younger men still discuss the topic accompanied by half-embarrassed giggles. It's thought of as amusingly naughty at best, and at worst, it's been a source of shame.

Women are reluctant to introduce the younger men they're dating to their parents or to their children for fear of being judged negatively. A woman may even worry about being called a "cougar," even if she's just four years older than her partner is. (If you're lucky enough to be unfamiliar with this stereotype, "cougar" is a particularly negative epithet for a woman who dates younger men. I'll discuss it in detail in Chapter 4.)

Of course, the woman in the relationship isn't the only one who suffers from the stigma. For an adult male, being ribbed by buddies that his girlfriend or wife is a "cradle-robber" can be insulting. He obviously entered into the relationship as a consenting adult with just as much interest as his partner. However, the preconceived notion claims that the woman chased him down, which puts the man in the position of having to argue that he, too, wanted the relationship or was himself the pursuer.

Before we delve any deeper, I want to be clear about what I mean by "females and younger men." In general, I'm referring to an age difference of ten years or less. In addition, I am referring to established, adult women in their mid-twenties and older (so that the men are twenty or older).

When the discussion turns to women dating men who are more than ten years younger (or more than ten years older, for that matter), generational differences and gaps in life experience come into play, which complicate the discussion. In some cases, relationships with more than a ten-year difference work and work well, but that's not the focus of this book.

Another way of measuring it is to think about the percentage of life that an age gap represents. If, for example, a 60 year-old woman dates a 55 year-old man, the five-year difference in their ages represents only about 8 percent of her life. No big deal, right? But if she were to date a 40 year-old man, the age difference would represent 33 percent of her life . . . and that's another story entirely.

So now that we know a little bit about the boundaries of the trend on a broader scale, let's look at how it plays out in individual women's lives. This book will show the sheer momentum of the FAYM trend, the number of women ignoring the stigma and loving whomever they happen to love and why they're finding that the female-and-younger-man relationship works financially, biologically, and psychologically.

Furthermore, you might be surprised to discover over the course of this book that in many ways, the FAYM relationship may actually work *better* than the traditional older-man-and-younger-woman pairing. So read on. You have nothing to lose—and 100 percent more opportunity for love to gain!

CHAPTER 3

How Dating and Marriage "Grew Up"

If we're only talking about couples that are not generations apart but simply have an age gap of a few
years, where does all the negativity come from?

Why do we think it's so unusual or just plain odd
to see a woman with a younger man? The truth is that
there were once fairly sound biological and economic

reasons for women to seek older partners. These reasons largely stemmed from societal inequality between the sexes, and as such, they aren't exactly defensible; however, in the reality of times past, they were logical. That's why women becoming comfortable with the idea of dating younger men is yet another step in the progression of equal rights for women.

What barriers was the FAYM relationship up against to begin with? For the vast majority of American history, women were not permitted to own land or hold assets. Ostensibly, for their own protection as the "softer sex," they had to exist under the care of men—if not their fathers or their husbands, then as wards of their extended families or of the church.

For a young man, coming into adulthood meant any number of things—joining the military, going to sea, gaining an advanced education, renting an apartment in the city, or learning a trade. Young men went through a period of striking out on their own, establishing themselves financially and personally as part of their coming of age.

For a young woman, coming of age meant moving out of her father's house and into her husband's house. A young woman's highest ambition of functioning as an adult in the world was to become a wife.

This reality persisted well into the 1960s. Though women were conferred the right to vote in 1920, it wasn't until the Women's Movement that they began claiming independent financial rights like holding their own credit cards or signing legal documents.

In fact, in the 1960s, my grandmother built a duplex building. She came up with the idea, found the land parcel, hired the architect and the contractor, and worked with them to create the development—but she wasn't allowed to sign for the loan because she was a woman. Her husband, who was not involved in the project in any other way (and as you will recall was much younger), was the one with financial credit in the family and, therefore, had to sign the paperwork for her.

Without being a wage earner, at best, a woman might hope to hide a small stash of bills in her purse, but all other aspects of her financial security—and, thus, her security in general—hinged on her husband. She owned no savings account, no property in her name, and no credit. Women were, as Simone de Beauvoir put it in 1949, "The Second Sex." They went from their father's house to their husband's with no sojourn into the world in between and no means of supporting themselves independently.

Young men typically didn't marry until they had completed enough education or gained enough experience in their careers to be able to support both themselves and their wives.

Young women, on the other hand, were eligible

to marry at eighteen and sometimes even younger. Often, the greater the age gap, the better the financial prospect for the woman; odds were that an older husband had a better job, was earning more, and was simply a more secure choice. Coupled with this was the fact that women had little reproductive control. Shortly after marriage—or shortly before, as the case may have been—they were pregnant and starting a family. In society's eyes, this was an ideal situation because, until very recently, women couldn't expect to bear children safely much past their twenties.

In fact, in the mid 1980s, I hosted a seminar for one of my hospital clients entitled "Over 30 and Pregnant?" as the idea of women purposely getting pregnant after thirty was new just twenty-five years ago. The seminar was mostly about the risks of pregnancy and a healthy birth at the very "old" age of 31 or more. So until fairly recently, for any man who hoped to have a family, there was a relatively small window of time during which women were eligible to become potential spouses and mothers. Any woman older than thirty was simply not a viable candidate.

Consequently, American society had been operating for centuries under two very strong forces—biological and financial—that locked both men and women into fairly strict age guidelines for choosing partners. Then, suddenly, over a very short period, a number of factors converged and turned this old paradigm on its head.

In 1960, the FDA approved the birth control pill for public use. The Free Love Movement gained popularity in 1967, and it was quickly overtaken by the unstoppable tide of the Feminist Movement in the 1970s.

For the first time, women had the option of postponing marriage for a number of reasons. First, the biological clock had slowed. Due to the pill, the consequences of sex prior to marriage were no longer as likely to result in pregnancy, and the ideals of free love made it increasingly socially acceptable to have sex with a "boyfriend." Therefore, as time went on, young people no longer felt pressure to rush into a legal contract as a prerequisite for physical intimacy.

Moreover, women who wanted to start a family were no longer constrained to a short period of fertility. With the simple advancement of standards in obstetrics and later the development of fertility drugs, it became perfectly safe for a woman to have children well into her thirties and forties and even beyond in some cases.

In the 1950s or 1960s, people wondered what had gone wrong if they ran into a 32 year-old woman who expected she would eventually have children but didn't have any yet. Today, she's more the standard than the exception. In fact, even sixteen years ago, my 30 year-old friend was the youngest person in her Lamaze class. Today, my friends in their twenties typically feel they are still too young for the responsibility and lifestyle of children and predominantly seek to begin their marriages in their late twenties, travel for a year of two, and then start their family.

The next part in the major change for women's roles was that having a career—and a high-responsibility, high-skill career at that—became an option for women for the first time. Education for women was no longer a question of "finishing" schools, where girls were prepped to become suitable wives and mothers. It was now something that young women could undertake for the same reasons as young men: preparation for a career or simply general self-betterment. Not surprisingly, women overwhelmingly opted to take that path, just as men had been doing for centuries.

As women began earning their own money, even if they weren't going to college, it became standard practice for them to move out of their parents' homes and into apartments to live independently for a period before entering into marriages and starting families. If a young woman didn't graduate from high school without getting pinned by her beau, or if she didn't graduate from college with her Mrs. degree, it was no longer the end of the road. She didn't have to go home to sit around her parents' house and hope that they'd uncover some friend with a long-lost second cousin with whom they could set her up. She had a career to focus on, her own home to keep, and an independent life to manage.

Being unmarried no longer carried the frightening financial and social consequences of being set adrift without a support network. Women were now supporting themselves, and as it turned out, they were just as successful as men were. This meant that their single years began stretching through their twenties into their thirties, and beyond. Even those who did marry often continued to work and contribute financially to their families.

That financial independence became a major factor in making no-fault divorce possible in the 1970s. For the first time, women had the option of leaving failing marriages because they weren't dependent on their husbands for support. It's not that there was a sudden spike in unhappy marriages in the 1970s; rather, it became socially acceptable and financially feasible to end marriages. People chose to do so in increasing numbers as we're so often reminded.

Beginning in the '70s, we started to see an increasing number of women who were single in the middle of their lives. In the past, it was only acceptable for a woman to be single in her youth, when hopefully she was doing everything in her power to secure a husband, and then again in her "old age," when her husband had passed away. She was essentially expected to live as a widow until the end of her life even if she'd been widowed in her late forties.

All of these shifts in the 1960s and 1970s created a cultural climate where it's simply no longer required for women to limit their choices in dating partners to men who are their age or older. We now live in a society where women spend much of their twenties earning bachelor's degrees and advanced degrees, after which they live alone and build careers. They also have fun doing it along with a majority of their peers. The average age for marriage in the United States continued to climb and is now 27 for men and 26 for women.

In addition, women don't need to search for spouses who are already well established. As we know, it's now commonplace for the woman to act as the family's primary breadwinner, whether putting her boyfriend or partner through graduate school or simply being the one with the higher-paying job. Women are also no longer pressured by biology to start their families young. Those who want children can and do wait until their thirties or even their forties.

According to the OECD, an international organization helping governments tackle the economic, social, and governance challenges of a globalized economy, in 1970, more than 60 percent of women in developed nations gave birth to their first child before the age of 25. Since that time, the first maternal age has been increasing. While in the United States, that age remains under 25 (it's currently 24.9 years of age), our country is number 14 on the list. In Sweden, a woman is now on average 27.9 years of age for the birth of her first child, and in New Zealand, the average age of a first-time mother is 29.9.

In addition, it's not just the "never-married" women who are single and dating. Due to divorce, many women also find themselves single again in their middle age with many more years of vibrancy and attractiveness ahead of them. Even those who don't divorce but are instead widowed later in life can now expect to live into their nineties and so may well want to begin dating again.

The last ingredient in the mix is that dating just doesn't mean what it used to mean. Dating used to be about selecting a spouse. If you discovered that your date probably wasn't someone you wanted to spend the rest of your life with, you were likely to move on quickly, but today, marriage isn't always the end goal. People often date simply for companionship and fun; they may not even have marriage in mind. The typical social calendar of a single woman these days might involve three different dates in one week and another three the next week.

Also, many women who have been widowed or divorced are not seeking a new spouse. Dating is not necessarily mating. It might just involve pleasant dinner conversation and someone with whom to attend movies.

Here's what it boils down to: There used to be legitimate biological and economic reasons for women to seek older partners. Those reasons are no longer relevant. On top of that, dating no longer carries the weight of "is this person my lifetime Mr. Right?" It's now about having a good time and enjoying another person's company.

So, why does it still feel weird for women to date younger men? The reality is that society's ideas of "normal" are tenacious, and they often persist long beyond their expiration date. Choosing to do something groundbreaking, particularly in the sensitive sphere of love and relationships, takes courage and some independent thinking. However, that kind of brave behavior is exactly what more and more women willingly displayed in recent years. The more women take a chance on men that are a few years younger than they are, the more it will become evident that an age difference of a few years is simply not an important factor.

Now that the trend has begun, it is likely that the FAYM relationship will become accepted very quickly.

The current generation—young people now in their teens—are not overly concerned with the social differences that used to raise their grandparents' blood pressure. They're friends with people of different sexual orientations and different races without even noticing those attributes. It seems easy to foresee a future in which this generation will pave an entirely different way for men and women of varying ages to relate. It's effortless to imagine a world in which young women from this generation reach their adulthood and ask, "Why would it make any difference if my boyfriend was in second grade when I was in fourth? We like the same music, remember the same videos, and even both got our first iPhones in high school."

I don't wish to imply that younger men are automatically more preferable than older men. In fact, I can't actually comment on that question from personal experience because I happened to marry a man a few years older than I am. But I didn't check his birth certificate before I accepted a first date with him. I thought he was handsome and that he had a great personality; ultimately, we fell in love. But is it possible that I, or any other woman, could meet a man a few years younger, who also might be handsome, have a great personality, and with whom she could eventually fall in love? The obvious answer is "of course!"

My point is that there are no drawbacks, no negatives to dating younger men, although earlier customs may have led us to believe that it's a strange thing to do. Once people reach adulthood, assuming that they are close enough in age that they have similar life experiences, a difference of a few years in either direction is simply irrelevant.

It's my hope that in reading this book, women will realize that they have absolute permission to look for love, companionship, or just a nice date where they might never have considered looking previously. So many single people, men and women, are truly hurting from loneliness. Why not double your chances of finding someone who really clicks with you?

Many prospects are your age or slightly older—but what if you opened the playing field to those who are slightly younger too? This ability to consider men up to ten years older and up to ten years younger gives each woman 100 percent more opportunity to find love.

Of course, we haven't reached total acceptance of the FAYM relationship yet. As an example, while sex is certainly a driving force in male-female relationships, it's not the only thing, and it's often not the main thing. So, is every woman seeking and finding love with a younger man by definition a cougar? The answer is no, and the reason why is in the next chapter.

CHAPTER 4

De-clawing the Cougar

Is it morally wrong to love a younger man? Judging by the old and still partially current societal stereotypes, it sure seems that way.

As unfounded and ridiculous as the stigma against women who date men younger than they are may be, it has dug its heels into our cultural subconscious with surprising tenacity. We are constantly bombarded with media images of "cougars" on the prowl—either as sexual victimizers or as desperate, botoxed has-beens. Overwhelmingly, the portrayal of these women seems to be to make them laughable, both to men and to other women. This certainly discourages women from joining in the FAYM trend.

But perhaps what we are witnessing is men's reaction to a changing world. In the early '70s, women who opened the door for themselves were called mean-spirited names by some men who were uncomfortable with women taking care of themselves. These men somehow felt threatened by a woman who didn't act meek and wasn't helpless when faced with the door to an office or restaurant.

Today, of course, women not only open the door for themselves on a regular basis but also will just as often open and hold the door for another woman or for a man. It's simply polite, no matter which gender is involved. This change in women opening up their choices for romantic partners, regardless of age, may also create a feeling of unease among men and among some women, too.

As we saw in Chapter 2, there's no longer any good reason to stand in the way of a woman dating a younger man. So why is the popular conception of these women so vicious? Who created the myth of the "cougar," and what is the benefit of propagating it?

In this chapter, I'll explore the cruel labels that society still places on women who date younger men—and I'll debunk them. It is not my wish to point an accusatory and indiscriminate finger at men. Throughout American history, particularly during the Women's Suffrage Movement and the later Feminist Movement, many men were invaluable and equal partners in women's struggle for recognition. However, we also can't deny that those movements were necessary in the first place because of constraints placed on women by a male-dominated society. Equality for women has been a long time coming (and still hasn't arrived in many respects) because men resisted it.

Why does women's equality make many men uncomfortable? I'd venture that it's for the same reason that any group in power resists the growing equality of minorities. Our human conception of power, whether accurate or not, tends to be that it's a zero-sum game. If men have control of a society, which is to say that they make decisions about both their own lives and women's lives, and women start demanding the right to make their own choices, men see that as reducing their sum total of power.

However, power is not quantifiable, and if women grow stronger, it doesn't automatically make men weaker. In fact, we can easily make the argument (and it has been made by countless politicians, economists, and sociologists) that the more equal rights a society grants to its minorities, the stronger the society will grow as a whole.

But as long as they're viewing their supply of power as finite, it makes perfect sense for men to resist women's equality. They've done so through the ages with all their might. The trouble for them was that in the early twentieth century, no good reason existed for why women shouldn't vote, and so eventually, their strained arguments were drowned out. In the 1960s and 1970s, no good reason existed for why women shouldn't receive equal education and equal job opportunities, and so again, men eventually lost the debate.

Finally, to extend the analogy, no good reason exists today for why women shouldn't have just as many opportunities to seek love and companionship as men, and so—eventually—men will have to acquiesce to the absolute normalcy of women dating younger men.

In the meantime, though, when men (or any group in power) sense that their control over others is threatened, the natural knee-jerk reaction is to search for any viable argument to shake off the threat. This is exactly what men did during the Women's Suffrage Movement. During the first quarter of the twentieth century, newspapers and countless editorials spewed all kinds of far-fetched arguments in favor of denying women the vote. Many men liked to cite women's physical inferiority as a reason why they shouldn't vote. They were seen, as I mentioned in Chapter 1, as the "softer sex," so frail that the act of voting in itself would simply be too much of a strain. Getting to the polling place, these men argued, would be exhausting, and even if a female voter made it there, she would have to suffer through long lines in extreme weather for which her fragile nature was not suited. In that rough and tumble men's world of politics, who is to guarantee that she might not be dragged into some kind of brawl, where she'd be helpless to defend herself?

This, of course, is to say nothing about her mental capacities. How could she be trusted, these men said, to go through the complex intellectual acrobatics necessary to discern one politician from another? Wouldn't the poor darling just pick the most handsome candidate or the one that kissed the most babies? Even if she did arrive by chance at a sensible decision, how could society impose on her slender fingers the weighty task of placing a check mark next to a candidate's name?

These arguments were put forth to the American people in all seriousness, and for decades, they went unchallenged. Now that women have the hard-won right to vote firmly under their belts, this blast from the past seems completely absurd. We think, *Was it even possible that men once thought that way? How did they ever get away with it?*

It's my hope that one day we'll say, "Cougar? What was *that* supposed to mean?" with just as much incredulity. Because just as no valid social or scientific foundation existed for denying women the vote, no valid reason can be found to deny women the opportunity to look for love or companionship. The reasons that men claim it's inappropriate for women to date younger men are just as absurd as arguing that they are too weak to walk down to the corner and pull a lever at their local polling place.

Now, I don't imagine that there's a group of men sitting around a darkened boardroom somewhere brainstorming vicious slander to use against women. In all likelihood, when they first started coming up with reasons why women shouldn't vote, they were wholly convinced of those reasons themselves. They didn't see themselves as part of a conspiracy to undermine women who had every right to be equal; they probably honestly thought they were acting in the weaker sex's—and society's—best interest.

My point, then, is not to accuse men of incorrigible oppression but rather to point out the depths of self-deception and callousness towards others that human beings are capable of when they feel their positions of power have been threatened. That's exactly why I don't think we can dismiss stereotypes like the "cougar" as harmless ribbing. They are orchestrated efforts, whether conscious or not, to keep women on lesser footing.

Let's examine some of these absurd arguments

and hurtful images that society has created to discourage women from dating younger men. First and most prevalent, there's the concept of the "cougar." She's a woman in her forties, fifties, sixties, or older; her gray hair dyed a garish platinum, her breasts augmented, and her face surgically re-mastered beyond any hope of natural human expression. She skulks in bars in an animal-print mini-skirt that clings to her less-than-perky derriere. She is a hunter, a sexually voracious predator, and her prey is the young, handsome, virile man in his twenties or thirties. If she "catches" him, he is an unsuspecting victim. The relationship is not mutual; he has been taken advantage of and preyed upon.

The cougar is an outgrowth of the older cultural image of Mrs. Robinson. In the 1967 film *The Graduate*, the character of Mrs. Robinson is a lonely alcoholic who first seduces the adrift, recent college graduate Ben Braddock and then slowly ensnares him in a web of control that very nearly destroys his life. She isn't actually any different from today's image of the cougar, except that at the time of the film's release, she was seen more as an eccentric character than a real threat to society because the trend of women dating younger men hadn't yet taken hold. However, she bears all the traits of the stereotype: Most importantly, she is significantly older than her chosen prey; her pursuit of the young man is purely sexual and even exploitative, and though she is still attractive, this quality is warped by her *scariness*: her alcoholism, her manipulative single-mindedness, and her obviously depressed and depressing existence.

This negative view of the cougar is not just that she's solely focused on using a younger man for her own pleasure but also that she is completely desperate and can't keep a man of her own age interested. These cultural images, Mrs. Robinson and her modern counterpart "the cougar," are extremes. They don't actually have anything to do with the current growing trend of women dating younger men.

Outside all the media hype, women are realizing that it's perfectly acceptable to date, fall in love with, and marry men who are anywhere from a few months to several years younger than they are. These relationships do not spring from a predator-prey dynamic, but rather they are mutually sought and mutually maintained. These relationships are not primarily about sex; they are about respect, companionship, and shared interests. In every aspect, they bear little resemblance to the nasty image of "cougar and prey," and yet, the women who embark on these relationships can hardly hope to escape this label.

Who is calling them "cougars"?

As I discussed above, the name calling probably originated with men in the same generation or older than the "cougars"—men who felt threatened by

the changing power dynamic implicit in a woman's increasing ability to choose her own partner and to choose from a wide field. The threat to these men is manifold.

First, they are so accustomed to being the older, more experienced, wealthier member of a couple—the leader—that they fear if the women are just as likely to be the older partner in a couple, they will have lost some power. They fear that being older automatically makes a person the instigator and the aggressor and that is supposed to be a man's role.

Therefore, they think it's a role reversal. They feel that men are supposed to be the aggressors in all things, from hunting beasts in the jungle to dictating budget cuts in the boardroom. If they surrender their position as *de facto* heads of all of their private relationships, then where does that leave them? Well, in reality, it makes them equals.

Men also perceive a second menace that leads them to brandish the "cougar" label: the threat of the younger man. These older men do not want to compete for a woman's attention with men as many as twenty years their junior. Fifty year-old men who are interested in 40 year-old women are used to competing with other 55 year-old men. Now, they suddenly find themselves up against 30 year-olds. It's a scary prospect, but it's one that women have contended with since the beginning of time.

We're all too familiar with the common tale of the male midlife crisis: At 50 years old, a husband buys a red convertible and runs off with a younger woman. Well, for the first time ever, his 48 year-old ex-wife has the power and means to respond in kind; she can buy her own red convertible, and—surprise— she may start dating a 43 year-old. No wonder the men don't like that potential scenario!

Other women form the second social group contributing to the tenacity of the "cougar" label. The women who participate in ridiculing their peers are likely also frightened; it may be they're frightened that they can't attract a younger man or that they themselves would be laughed at by other men and women. These women might see their friends involved in perfectly healthy, mutual relationships with younger men, and they might even be curious about what it would be like to be in such a relationship themselves, but at the same time, they see how much societal pressure their friends face.

They don't want to be the ones being laughed at—so they participate in the laughing, to greater or lesser degrees, out of fear and jealousy. Unfortunately, for these women, the joke is often on them. Once they point out a supposed "cougar," the worst thing they can find to say about her is, "Oh . . . she looks like she's having a great time with a man who likes her." What's the big tease there?

Then, another surprising group of women don't like "cougars." Much to my surprise, one night while I was out, an attractive woman in her twenties told me she'd been warned about the cougars, coming along with all their good looks, expensive outfits, and lots of confidence and attracting the best looking 30-something men away from the much more insecure young women!

Finally, some women who actually *do* fit the cougar mold (in as much as their relationships with younger men are primarily about sex) propagate the stereotype.

Any time there is a shift in society, and behaviors that were previously unacceptable become acceptable, there tends to be a swing towards the extreme before things start to even out. Many women realize for the first time, "Oh, I *am* attractive to these younger men—I haven't died just because I turned 40! A 36 year-old man thinks I'm pretty." In turn, they overreact to their newfound power, and they chase younger men just for fun.

For these women, while the actual appeal is often still the boost to their confidence by proving their desirability, sex is the main approach, which, when it comes to women, is something that we continue to be extremely uncomfortable with as a society. Traditionally, women aren't supposed to go to bars to find men to sleep with—men of any age. It simply isn't lady-like, and as liberated as they might be, even most women who engage in this behavior sure wouldn't want it brought up in front of their family or coworkers. If a woman has gone out and pursued sex, particularly with a stranger, she is made to feel quite shameful. Society does its best to keep other women from following her example. Hence, the media images of cougars become even more predatory and warped than any of these women would actually appear.

The interesting thing is that the predator-prey dynamic is largely absent from women's interactions with younger men, even the ones closest to the cougar stereotype who are only looking for sex. Why is this? Because what society is reluctant to recognize is that younger men actually *are* attracted to older women—of their own volition, without being coerced, manipulated, or preyed upon.

In fact, in the common vernacular, you'll rarely hear the younger man labeled the cougar's "prey." More often than not, he's called a "cougar hunter," which puts him back on the aggressor's path and makes catching a cougar another conquest.

While male political candidates push Viagra for men who are no longer physically capable of easily having sex, society has continued its best attempt to subvert older women's sexuality to make it seem unnatural, perverse, and predatory, even labeling these women beasts of prey.

But an important detail in the FAYM relationship: young men are obviously willing participants and, most often, are the instigators.

As much as society might try to keep these women confined to the roles of either motherhood or spinsterhood that age called for in past generations, younger men *do* find older women desirable. Remember, we're discussing situations in the FAYM relationship in which a 37 year-old male finds a 41 year-old female attractive. She's older than he is, but she's not his mother's age.

When we think about these nasty labels, perhaps the most important thing to note is that while the word *cougar* might be used by all kinds of members of society, male and female, who feel threatened by or uncomfortable with this societal trend, you'd be hard pressed to find a member of an actual FAYM couple using the word. Women who date younger men do not call themselves "cougars," nor do they think of themselves in that way. Men who date older women do not call their partners "cougars," but rather they call those women their girlfriends, significant others, or wives. This is because they recognize that their relationships are not about only sex. They are about mutuality and are just as normal, commonplace, and human as any other relationship.

Perhaps, two people met at the market when they both reached for the same avocado; they went out to dinner, discovered they enjoyed each other's company, and started a relationship. Maybe the man happened to be younger than the woman was. But he'd never accuse her of "trapping" him, and she'd never congratulate herself for a successful "hunt."

Furthermore, "cougar" is a strictly one-sided label. Is there any epithet for a man who likes dating younger women? No. He's just a man—a regular guy. But being called a "cougar" is, decidedly, a bad thing. It's a bad thing in the eyes of men *and* women—a negative label on all fronts.

One must recognize that the label has little basis in reality. The real trend of women dating younger men is not about Mrs. Robinsons throwing themselves at innocent college boys who would prefer to date their daughters. It's not about cougars with insatiable sexual appetites preying on unsuspecting young men at nightclubs.

What's really happening is that a single woman is recognizing that she might have just as much in common with a man five years her junior as she does with a man five years her senior. Why should she limit herself? Because society says so? Because hurtful labels and stereotypes float around and seek to shame her? Of course not!

Women didn't let unfounded attempts to undermine them keep them from demanding the right to vote, the right to equal education, or the right to work. The same holds true in this case.

Cougar stereotype or not, women are dating younger men in unprecedented numbers, and eventually, old-fashioned thinkers are going to have to catch up. If so many people in society drag their heels and cling to unfounded stigmas like the cougar slur—how do we prod them into the twenty-first century? One place Americans have looked through the ages for the latest trendsetting is Hollywood. If it's okay by Hollywood, chances are it'll soon be okay by America.

In the next chapter, we'll peak into celebrity FAYM relationships and discuss how these high-profile couples helped pave the way for mainstream FAYM acceptability.

CHAPTER 5

What Happens in Hollywood Never Stays in Hollywood

Whenever a new social trend pops up in American culture, the first place you'll see it gain acceptance is Hollywood. We look to Hollywood to tell us what's new and hot; often, whether it's conscious or not, we follow suit.

Within a month after Paris Hilton bought her

Chihuahua, almost everyone on the street walked identical pups—or carried them in their handbags. Who could forget those years in the 1990s when every woman in America had Jennifer Aniston's (Rachel's) haircut?

Of course, a thousand and one books have been written on the topic of our obsession with celebrities and what makes us revere and revile them. But it doesn't take any kind of in-depth sociological study to observe that celebrities' lives of glamour, wealth, and popularity are attractive to us, and it makes us feel good if we can mirror those lives in some way, even if it's just by buying a pair of shoes. (Especially if we're buying Manolos like Sarah Jessica Parker's gorgeous, happy character on *Sex and the City*.)

Sometimes our fascination with celebrity lifestyles runs much deeper than fashion trends. It's often through the highly visible—and highly scrutinized—lives of celebrities that social trends first receive public attention, then, acceptance, and even approval. Unlike superficial fashion trends, however, celebrities aren't necessarily the first ones to start certain social behaviors that the rest of us eagerly copy. Often, they simply lend more visibility to things that mainstream Americans have already been doing for some time, but doing in secret or in shame.

Celebrities bring "alternative" or simply new kinds of lifestyles and relationships into the public eye. Because Hollywood personalities are so visible, seeing them engage in new social trends openly and without shame plays a huge part in those trends becoming increasingly less shocking to us and more acceptable.

To pick a relatively uncontroversial example, the first women—from girl-next-door Americans to actresses and models—who wore miniskirts in the '60s generated a lot of buzz, but as more and more magazine covers featured the style, it quickly ceased to shock. Now it's so commonplace that it's almost unusual to see a young woman in southern California who *isn't* in a miniskirt on a hot August day. There are endless examples of Hollywood bearing the torch for subjects more touchy than where a woman's hemline falls.

Even though human beings have been cohabitating and having children out of wedlock since the beginning of time, celebrities' high-profile relationships played an enormous role in the fact that these living arrangements no longer make us flinch.

Jerry Hall, an American model who had a long and much-talked-about romance with rocker Mick Jagger, never married him although the couple had four children together. They lived together long enough to have a common law marriage and eventually had an unofficial Balinese wedding ceremony, but they never chose to wed officially and legally. The fact that celebrities like Jerry Hall are willing to say openly, *Sure, we're living together, and we have children, but we don't have any plans to get married*, has done much to lend credence to the practice of cohabitation in the U.S. It's no longer something that raises eyebrows.

Jerry Hall certainly strikes us all as a woman who could, if she desired, find a handsome man who would marry her. This fact further validates that it's her choice to live with someone to whom she's not married. It doesn't strike us as a situation in which she is "stuck."

The same holds true for women becoming single parents. Minnie Driver gave birth to a baby boy in September 2008 and opted not to marry the father. In fact, she remains guarded about the father's identity but has admitted the pregnancy was unplanned. However, she doesn't intend to continue a relationship with the father. The *New York Post* quoted her as saying, "It's great to be an independent creature. Today you don't need a man anymore. In the old days, if you had a baby without marriage, people would put you out. I'm very into feeling this female thing."

Here is a gorgeous, rich, famous woman who could obviously marry just about anybody she wanted, but instead, she decided to raise her child on her own. She's certainly not the first woman to make that choice, but because she—and celebrities like her—

does so willingly and openly, mainstream women are now realizing that they don't have to feel ashamed if they choose not to enter an unhappy attachment just because they are pregnant.

In fact, many celebrity women choose to circumvent men altogether by adopting. Meg Ryan, who is unmarried, adopted a baby girl from China in 2006. Of the experience, Ryan told *Redbook*, "This is the best time in my whole life. I'm happy in my skin, I'm happy in my home, I'm happy in my career. I'm just very satisfied all around. I don't feel like I'm living anybody else's life, or anybody else's idea of what I should be doing, and it just feels very good."

Sheryl Crow followed the same path about a year after her much publicized broken engagement with Lance Armstrong. She adopted a baby boy in 2007 and raised him as a single mother. She takes her son with her on tour, and she told *People* magazine, "He's been doing it since he was two months old. He's been around the world. He's really the rock star—and I'm his sidekick now."

Whether single mothers make the "right" or "wrong" choice is still an argument that some people can and do have, but the important thing to note is that it's simply not shocking anymore.

Whether living together without being married is "right" or "wrong" is still an argument, but it is no longer shocking.

Once celebrities engage in a social trend and do it visibly because their public lifestyles leave them little choice, what they're doing becomes increasingly acceptable. As people realize that certain choices are okay for celebrities, they think, "Why shouldn't it be okay for me, too?" That is exactly what we are starting to see with the trend of women dating younger men.

For several years now, increasing numbers of women in Hollywood have been choosing younger men to date and even marry. These women are sophisticated, successful, and in great shape. It's not a stretch to imagine that they could get just about any man they want, but they are choosing younger men. So rather than thinking that these relationships are weird, inappropriate, or simply liaisons of convenience, Americans start to discover that they are the perfectly natural result of two adults meeting, finding that they enjoy each other's company, and deciding to embark on a relationship.

Whether a female marrying a younger male is "right" or "wrong" is not only unworthy of shock, but it's also happening on such a large scale that most people may be unaware of couples whose ages are different.

Dating someone younger (even much younger) is something, of course, that male celebrities have been doing in Hollywood all along. Men like Hugh Hefner popularized the image of an older man with a nineteen year-old on each arm. The beautiful, young girlfriend became the ultimate status symbol in American culture. It was perhaps somewhat risqué to see a white-haired gentleman with a blonde bombshell, but nobody really raised an eyebrow. That kind of relationship was well within the bounds of what was expected from a lavish Hollywood lifestyle, and it didn't threaten the American conception of traditional gender roles.

But then, Cher started dating younger men in the 1980s, most famously Tom Cruise (sixteen years younger) and Val Kilmer (thirteen years younger). She was one of the first women to take this step, at least publicly. Interestingly enough, the age difference didn't seem to be what fans were most excited about. They just wanted to hear about two famous people getting together, and birth dates simply weren't huge news.

Before these relationships, Cher had married Gregg Allman of The Allman Brothers Band in the '70s. What most people don't pay much attention to or think of as particularly remarkable about their relationship is that Allman was born about a year and a half after Cher. If a few months' difference isn't gossip worthy for Cher, why should it be such a source of embarrassment for mainstream American women?

Once Cher broke down the barrier, more and more celebrity women began publicly declaring through their dating choices that they weren't going to be constrained by a double standard. If the men of Hollywood could get away with using teenage girlfriends as little more than status symbols, why should female celebrities feel ashamed of mutual and loving relationships with adult men who happened to be a few years younger than they were?

In the late '80s, Susan Sarandon began a long-term partnership with Tim Robbins, who is twelve years her junior. Regardless of whether you're her biggest fan, you'd be hard pressed to call Susan Sarandon a ravenous predator.

A decade later, Madonna became involved with her personal trainer Carlos Leon for several years, and the couple had a child, Lourdes. Leon is eight years younger than Madonna is, but to most of her fans, that wasn't the interesting part of the relationship. Most people were enthralled with the fact that Madonna, perhaps the biggest pop celebrity of her generation, fell in love with a man who was completely unknown to the rest of the world. Their relationship developed out of working together and sharing interests; they spent time together and eventually realized they were in love. This relationship was clearly not driven by external, superficial factors. Madonna didn't care about whether Leon was rich, famous, older, or more powerful than she was. They simply fell in love.

Although her relationship with Leon didn't ultimately last, it's clear that Madonna didn't blame it on the age difference because she has gone on to have two more high-profile relationships with younger men.

In 2000, she married the celebrated British film director Guy Ritchie, who is ten years younger than she is. The couple divorced in 2008, but again, the ending of that liaison didn't cause her to shun younger men.

She has also been involved with the Yankees baseball star Alex Rodriguez, or A-Rod, who is seventeen years her junior. The Madonna/A-Rod relationship is particularly striking because it's so iconic in our culture. A major actress and singer coupled with a major sports figure . . . remember Marilyn Monroe and Joe DiMaggio? But Joe was twelve years older than Marilyn. Now Madonna is turning the paradigm on its head, but that's hardly the reason that the alliance creates so much buzz. Far more titillating is just the fact that two mega stars are together.

Another important thing to notice about the Madonna/A-Rod relationship is that it hasn't threatened A-Rod as a symbol of ultimate masculinity in any way. None of his fans would say that Madonna preyed on him or robbed his cradle. "Helpless victim" is the last thing that comes to mind when you look at those biceps. More likely, the men who look up to him are saying, "Wow, he's with Madonna? Good for him!" A-Rod sends the message to younger men that dating an older woman isn't going to make them any less manly or powerful.

Another example is Roger Federer. Federer recently married his long-time girlfriend, Mirka, a former tennis pro herself. The couple welcomed twin baby girls into the world in the summer of 2009. The big surprise? Federer is three years younger than Mirka. But at the time of this book's writing, Federer still ranks as the world's number one professional tennis player by the Association of Tennis Professionals. Some professionals and commentators have even dubbed him the greatest tennis player of all time.

Does his relationship with a woman slightly his senior compromise his athleticism or his manliness? Not in the least! In fact, most of his fans celebrate the fact that he has been with Mirka for nearly nine years since the two met competing for Switzerland, their home country, in the 2000 Olympics. People applaud him for picking a lasting relationship with a woman possessing down-to-earth, girl-next-door beauty and charm rather than flitting from one shallow relationship with one super model to the next as is all too common in the celebrity world of professional sports.

Another recent Hollywood union of an older woman and a younger man is, of course, Demi Moore and Ashton Kutcher, who are separated by fifteen years. Their relationship is another prime example of a beautiful, iconic female celebrity choosing a younger man. It flies in the face of the stereotype of older women being undesirable and, therefore, needing to lure much more attractive younger men into their clutches. Hardly anyone would disagree that Demi Moore fulfills our society's high standards for physical attractiveness. Most men, whether in older or younger generations, would think Ashton Kutcher caught a lucky break rather than suspect he was somehow hoodwinked.

So many FAYM relationships exist among celebrities that one hardly knows where to begin. There's Victoria Beckham (also known as Posh Spice) and David Beckham

Jane Fonda and Ted Turner

Helen Hunt and Hank Azaria

Nicole Kidman and Keith Urban

Tracy Pollan and Michael J. Fox

Kelly Ripa and Mark Consuelos

Julia Roberts and Danny Moder

Of course, since this is Hollywood, any or all of these relationships may be ancient history by the time you read this book. But the point is clear: There is no bias among celebrities against dating or marrying younger men. Unlike Vegas, what happens in Hollywood radiates from Hollywood to the rest of society.

This is also not intended to imply that it's only appropriate for extraordinarily beautiful women to date younger men. In the real world, not every woman is a "genetic celebrity" like those who survive the winnowing process by which Hollywood and the music industry select their stars. But it is a great wake-up call that tells us there's no reason to impose some arbitrary expiration date on a woman's desirability.

People will be attracted to whomever they please, and checking a birth certificate isn't going to factor into that process.

In fact, in the March 2003 issue of *Ebony*, legendary singer Gladys Knight, who is married to a man 13 years her junior, is quoted as saying "Look with your heart, not your eyes." Ms. Knight married William McDowell who she had known for 14 years before they began dating. Due to their religious beliefs, they didn't have their first kiss until their wedding day.

Celebrities don't just lend credence to new social trends through their real dating lives. You can also put a finger on society's pulse by checking what celebrities are doing in their fictional incarnations in movies and on TV.

It used to be that the only films that touched on the topic of older women with younger men were cautionary tales, such as *The Graduate*, which I discussed in Chapter 3, or *Breakfast at Tiffany's*, where an older woman pays Audrey Hepburn's young love interest for his "services." Film examples of healthy relationships between older women and younger men didn't exist, but rather the women depicted were all exploitative, and their sexuality was depicted as disgusting.

In the last decade or so, however, there has been a virtual barrage of films about women dating younger men, and many have told positive stories.

It's worth noting that although my focus in this book is on age gaps of only a few years, most of these movies deal with relationships where the age gap is extreme, often greater than fifteen years. This is perhaps simply because extreme circumstances make for more engaging stories. Who would pay $10.50 to watch 45 year-old Sue go on uneventfully pleasant dates with 42 year-old Sam, get married, and raise children (his, hers, and theirs) together? The cinema isn't exactly a microcosm for the greater part of this American trend.

However, in portraying women in relationships with younger men, sometimes much younger men, Hollywood does a lot to bring this sort of couple into our comfort zone and to remind us that women don't automatically cease to be desirable and datable on their fortieth (or fill in the blank with any arbitrary number) birthday.

Something's Gotta Give, which was released in

2003, shows the lighter side of the FAYM relationship. In this film, Diane Keaton's character Erica is a divorced playwright who is still vivacious at 56—so much so that she catches the eye of Julian, a young doctor played by Keanu Reeves. At first, she is completely astonished; she can't believe that he would like her. She still reels from her husband leaving her, more or less, because he wanted to find someone younger. But Julian thinks she is pretty, loves her work, and admires her. He's all in.

By the climax of the film, after they have been dating for several months, he's ready to propose. But we never get to see how their relationship might have turned out because Erica has been in love all along with Harry, played by Jack Nicholson, who at 63 is the more age-appropriate choice. In the end, she chooses Harry.

The movie is a clever inversion of the typical older man/younger woman theme (Harry first arrives on the scene because he's dating Erica's 30-something daughter). Even though Erica eventually makes the more conventional choice in love, she makes it for love and not because she feels constrained by social expectations. The implication is that her relationship with Julian is perfectly normal, mutual, and balanced and could succeed were it not for that one nagging detail—Erica loves someone else more.

The same is true of the movie version of the

hit show *Sex and The City*. In the movie, Samantha is in California with her much younger man whom she adores. The problem that finally separates them doesn't come from their age difference but that he's very involved in his career, and Samantha is simply bored and alone while he's at work, missing her friends and busier life in New York.

If *Something's Gotta Give* ultimately goes in a safe direction by pairing a 56 year-old woman with a 63 year-old man, *How Stella Got Her Groove Back* goes out on a limb and paints a portrait of a successful and (we can assume) enduring relationship between an older woman and a younger man.

Stella, played by Angela Bassett, a successful stockbroker in her forties is persuaded by a girlfriend to treat herself to a vacation in Jamaica. While there, she meets the resort worker Winston Shakespeare (Taye Diggs), who is 20 years old. At first, she thinks the sparks between them are just a fling and that a real relationship could never work, but by the end of the film, Stella realizes that she and Winston share something real—they love each other.

The film was a tremendous critical and popular success; it won the 1999 NAACP Image Award for Outstanding Motion Picture and grossed over $37 million. If that's any indication, it would seem that moviegoers weren't at all bothered by the idea of a happy ending between a woman and a younger man.

As Oscar Wilde's famous saying goes, "Life imitates art far more than art imitates life." I'm not suggesting that any of these movies or the personal lives of the celebrities who make them will incite Americans to do things they wouldn't otherwise do. However, the fact that these movies appear in greater numbers and that they come from major producers and achieve significant popular success indicates that people are much more at ease with this trend and are ready to acknowledge it in popular culture. The more they see it given credence on the big screen, the more comfortable women will be in entering into relationships with younger men.

Reactions to the film *Brokeback Mountain* represent a similar phenomenon. It's not that going to see *Brokeback Mountain* turned otherwise straight men gay. But the fact that a gay couple was portrayed in a major Hollywood film—and that the film received critical praise and success in theatres with both gay and straight audiences—was momentous for the gay community. The movie doesn't suggest that everything in a gay relationship will be easy as pie; in fact, it shows the men struggling and the community around them struggling. But the message that the audience can take away is, simply, that sometimes people who love each other are the same gender. Having that acknowledged in a major, popular way validated the gay community.

The much lighter television show *Will & Grace* provides another example of the same phenomenon. It opens a window for straight and gay audiences to accept that Will is "just like every other guy," except that he's gay.

By the same token, *Guess Who's Coming to Dinner*, the classic film starring Sidney Poitier about a white woman bringing her black fiancé and his parents home to meet her family, helped bring interracial marriage into the public eye as something that could be discussed openly rather than hidden.

Much more recently, *Guess Who* (starring, coincidentally, Ashton Kutcher) dealt with the inverse situation: a young black woman bringing her white boyfriend home. By the time *Guess Who* came out in 2005, it was sort of an amusing, cute scenario; it no longer held weighty social implications. Society has confronted the issue of love between different races and digested it. For the most part, it is now perfectly acceptable in mainstream culture.

As more and more celebrity women date younger men openly and as more films bring relationships with age gaps into public consciousness, the same level of acceptance will develop. In fact, it's already increasing. It's as if Hollywood rolls out the red carpet for things that Americans are already doing. What used to be secret and a little naughty becomes increasingly acceptable as it gains attention in Hollywood. The men and women in these relationships already know that they are involved in something normal, acceptable, and loving—but it helps to know they're not alone.

We've now discussed why economics used to constrain women to marry men older than they were. We've seen how through education, equality, and medical advances, those reasons disappeared. We've also looked at why a social change had to pass psychological hurdles in order to grow. In this chapter, we reviewed what FAYM relationships are like in their most public incarnations—amongst celebrities.

But what about FAYM relationships at their most private . . . in the bedroom? In the next part of the book, I'll discuss the many perks of FAYM relationships that most people simply haven't previously considered.

PART II:

WHY IT'S GREAT TO BE FAYMous

CHAPTER 6

The FAYM Couple in Bed

Okay, it's time for the moment of truth. Do FAYM relationships work in the bedroom? The answer is, overwhelmingly, *yes*.

In fact, much evidence suggests that this might be the most ideal combination for physical fireworks. In this chapter, I'll explore why from both a cultural and scientific viewpoint—with some input from sex therapy and education expert Alicia Koberstein.

There's no denying it: Physical attraction is an important factor in any romantic relationship, no matter what the partners' ages. In the very beginning of a relationship, it's the *only* factor. A man sees a woman across the room at a party, and with only her appearance to go on, he decides he wants to introduce himself, or a woman meets a new coworker for the first time, and there's that spark of attraction. Immediately, her interaction with him shifts. Something more is possible in the relationship.

Even for people who are comfortable meeting other singles through blind dates set up by their friends, Internet dating sites, and matchmaking services, physical attraction is still the crux at the start of a relationship. Attraction happens on many levels. "Chemistry" is not as simple as it might seem. Certainly not every wedding photo portrays a suave, handsome, well-built man.

Of course, for any individual, much mystery surrounds that "spark" of physical attraction. Whether a person fits society's standards for attractiveness is completely irrelevant, so long as he or she is attractive to his/her partner in particular. No formula predicts how and when attraction will strike. Most women say that they value a sense of humor in their dating partners. They also look for kindness—the ability to be gentle and understanding of their needs. If a man has these qualities, his girlfriend might become more and more attracted to him, even if she wasn't necessarily thunderstruck on the first date.

Until fairly recently in American history, both men and women tended to "let themselves go." As they aged, the pull of gravity and a few extra pounds were just accepted. But today, with advances in science and medicine and with increasing knowledge about nutrition and exercise, women in their fifties look better than women a few generations ago looked in their thirties.

In the 1950s, the neighborhood wife and mother who went out jogging past white picket fences would have been seen as eccentric at best. Women weren't supposed to exert themselves; at the very most, they stayed in shape by pushing a stroller around the block.

At the same time though, a woman's two most marketable features in terms of finding a husband were her family's social status and her looks. Men had a little more leeway; if they weren't exactly stunners, they could court based on their careers, their wit, or their education. It was only natural that women were encouraged to marry as young as possible when they were at the height of their attractiveness and could catch the best possible man.

It was only natural for men to look for young, pretty wives, since women's other assets weren't held in much esteem. Consequently, physical attraction was yet another factor that bolstered the social mores of men dating and marrying younger women. It's yet another factor no longer applicable in contemporary society.

It's also not what always happened. Men may believe that initial attraction tends to be cut and dry. But attraction, of course, is in the eyes of the beholder. While women today certainly take better care of their health than perhaps their grandparents did, not everyone looks like a celebrity. Not every woman in the world who was pursued by an older man was necessarily in great shape nor beautiful in the classic sense. In fact, we all know women who we may not personally consider attractive who meet and marry men we think wouldn't be attracted to them either—but obviously are.

However, the reality of the "looks" department has changed in women's favor. Women are health conscious and exercise enthusiastic well beyond middle age. All that yoga, Pilates, jogging, spinning, belly dancing, or you-name-it is paying off. This is, of course, not to mention the little extra help many seek from cosmetic surgery.

Today, it's perfectly natural for a woman who is 40 to be attractive to a man who is 30 or for a woman who is 50 to be attractive to a man who is 40—and so on into the golden years.

The idea of a man being drawn to an older woman

is no longer laughable or icky but very real. Similarly, a woman finding a man unattractive because he has let himself go and become out of shape as he has aged is quite well understood.

Remember the men worried about a woman's ability to pick from a larger age group? Part of that may be due to the increased pressure it puts on older men to stay in shape, eat right, and consider cosmetic surgery to stay "in the game."

I absolutely don't intend to imply that FAYM relationships only work when the woman has the genes and workout regimen of Madonna. My point is that the old stereotype that women are only desirable when they are nubile and virginal no longer holds water in contemporary culture.

Because of the Women's Movement, our society started to recognize that a woman's contribution isn't limited to pretty, teenage dimples. It's now acceptable for us to think of women of any age as attractive and sexual beings—no matter their shapes, sizes, or whether they fit the cookie-cutter mold of classical beauty.

FAYM relationships work today because it has become acceptable for women to participate with men as peers, and so they can be desirable not only for their looks but for their intelligence, wit, humor, kindness, or any number of things—just as men have always been.

Another cultural shift occurring in the last century that supports the FAYM relationship is simply the newfound acceptability of female sexuality. Up to the early 1900s, it was uncomfortable to think of women as capable of enjoying sex. Women were either blushing young virgins or nurturing mothers, and sexuality wasn't compatible with either persona. Men considered sex to be a marital duty for women; something they simply had to endure to please their husbands and bring children into the world.

Of course, some women did enjoy sex anyway, but at best, they didn't talk about it much, and at worst, they thought of their pleasure as an embarrassing accident.

As I discussed in Chapter 3, the Sexual Revolution and the birth control pill gave that old paradigm a real run for its money. Initially, some women took the new behavior way over the edge by attending key-swapping parties and being just as physical in seeking sex as men had always been. That type of constant and random partnering is, of course, no longer something women largely do. But we now live in a culture where we all know and accept that women are sexual beings. Not only is that fine with us (or the overwhelming majority of us), but we celebrate it. Look at the tremendous success of the HBO series *Sex and the City* or the fact that women's magazines can unabashedly trumpet headlines like "Six Positions That Bring Women The Most Pleasure" in the middle of the supermarket checkout aisle.

One of the effects of this sexual liberation for women is that finding a sex partner has become a legitimate reason for a woman to date. Perhaps since the beginning of time and certainly in the modern era, acquiring sex has been a major reason why *men* date. In fact, the AARP survey I cited in Chapter 1 found that five times as many men as women say that fulfilling their sexual needs is their single most important reason for dating. (For both genders, however, in the 40-plus age group surveyed, this reason still trails far behind "having someone to talk to/do things with.") In general, a man dating as a pathway to sex has been reinforced as early as adolescence.

While the high school prom is about romance for young women, young men often go in the hopes of "getting lucky."

Later in their lives, dating becomes a way for men to secure a partner to have sex with on a regular basis; it's just easier and safer than having to look for someone new at the bar every Friday night.

Women can now adopt the same reasoning without feeling ashamed. Of course, for men and women, sex is rarely the *only* reason for entering into a relationship. But many women today might feel that marriage is simply not their goal at this time. Perhaps, they feel they are too young to get married, or a woman may be uninterested in marriage because she was severely hurt in a previous relationship. A divorced woman may be attempting to discover who she is as "just me" or want to devote as much of herself as possible to raising her children from a previous marriage.

For whatever reason, marriage or remarriage might not be on some women's immediate horizon, but the idea of a celibate decade or even lifetime is certainly not appealing.

So, they date—partly to have someone to go to dinner with, but also to have someone to go to bed with. That's no longer shameful—in fact, women across the U.S. (and abroad) were partly so delighted with *Sex and the City* because they could relate to the common experience of dishing with girlfriends at Sunday brunch about last night's hot date.

The trend of women dating younger men is a natural extension of the newfound acceptability of female sexuality in our culture. If it's acceptable for women to list sex as a factor in their dating lives, it only follows that they shouldn't be restricted by arbitrary rules about to whom they can and can't be attracted.

Here, we find a perfect storm of cultural factors. Women may find themselves single in their thirties, forties, fifties, sixties, seventies, or eighties. Women possess the means to stay fit and attractive well into their middle age and beyond; society is beginning to recognize that looks are not (and may never have been) the be-all and end-all of women's desirability, *and* women now hold the reins to their own healthy and active sex lives. These factors add up to an environment ripe for physical chemistry between women and younger men.

So, the attraction is there, and it's increasingly socially acceptable, but how does it fare when push comes to shove (so to speak)? Do these relationships stand a chance in the bedroom? I posed the question to sex therapist Alicia Koberstein and learned that, on a purely physiological level, pairing a woman with a younger man is actually the ideal heterosexual coupling.

Human sexuality is, of course, a complicated physiological phenomenon, but scientists tend to agree that men reach their sexual peak in their late teens, while women peak in their mid to late thirties. "Peak" in this case refers to libido, but also to the sexual response cycle—the time it takes to go from arousal to climax to resolution.

When men are in their thirties, their testosterone levels often begin decreasing, which means that in relationships where the couple is the same age, women are gearing up as men are winding down. While I haven't seen this depicted in Hollywood, I've certainly heard about it from girlfriends at the gym.

According to Koberstein, in the early stages of

the relationship, the older man might want sex more often than the younger woman does if she's in her twenties. By the time her libido picks up, her partner is already on the downside of the curve. The result is a relationship that never hits a perfect overlap in sexual appetites.

The discrepancy in libidos becomes even more pronounced in relationships where the man is older than the woman is. An age gap favoring the woman, on the other hand, could mean that a couple is more in sync, both in terms of their desire for sex and in their ability to go through the sexual response cycle at about the same pace.

This is not to say that 35 year-old women should be looking for 17 year-old boyfriends. Koberstein notes that virility is not all that's important in making love, and sometimes it can even be a drawback. A man with some experience is going to have a lot more finesse and ability to communicate nonverbally with his partner than a young man in his late teens or early twenties who might just be thinking about going at it like a bull at a gate.

What seems to be the ideal situation is a relatively small age gap, perhaps five to ten years, which would simply ensure that the couple is physiologically compatible for a longer overlapping period.

However, Koberstein quickly reminded me that physiology is hardly the whole story when it comes

to human sexual behavior. Psychological influences like emotional attachment deeply affect our desires. She suggested that in addition to the positive factors in FAYM relationships for physiological chemistry, FAYM sexual relationships might benefit from a number of psychological factors as well.

Women have an instinctual tendency to nurture that can be allowed more freedom to flourish with a younger partner than with an older one who might automatically dominate. For the woman, many positive feelings can be associated with having the opportunity to take the lead and share her experience. The man can gain the gratification of learning from a partner who knows her admittedly complex desires and body well and has the confidence to make requests and offer guidance.

It's no secret that men are often frustrated by women's sexual complexity, which can be even more baffling with a young female partner who is still a mystery even to herself. It might be extremely refreshing for a man to be with an experienced woman who can cut to the chase and tell him outright, "Here is what I need." Even with an age gap of only a few years, these feelings might be unconsciously at play, adding to the compatibility of the younger-male relationship.

Another positive aspect of these relationships, Koberstein points out that a younger man can help a woman rediscover the fun and playfulness of sex.

For women who have gone through bad relationships, sex can have weighty, intense connotations. For senior women returning to dating after losing a spouse of many years, the idea of having a new partner might seem scary. It's easy for anyone, male or female, to begin to attach a lot of significance to sexual performance, to overanalyze, and to lose touch with simply enjoying the feelings in the moment.

But to Koberstein, "the bedroom is a playground, not a proving ground." She points out that the sense of vitality a younger man brings to a relationship might help a woman to feel youthful and hopeful and to remember that laughter is allowed in a sexual relationship.

Another psychological plus for a FAYM relationship is that it can make a woman feel sexy—not just to her lover but to the outside world. No relationship exists in a vacuum, and part of what's sexy about dating a younger man might be the way he makes his girlfriend feel out on the town or in front of her friends. Just as men have found when out with younger women, it bolsters her feelings of confidence and self-worth to know that she is attractive to this young virile person—and to be able to display this attractiveness in public. Nothing is inherently unhealthy about that; in fact, it's good for any relationship to have feelings of pride about your partner.

On the other hand, Koberstein does warn that as age gaps increase, it becomes easier for less healthy sexual motivators to creep into play. Relationships in which the man is significantly older than the woman often involve an unhealthy power skew in which the man is able to satisfy a need to dominate his much younger, less experienced partner. The inverse relationship, where the woman is the significantly older partner, might be about filling a void such as empty nest syndrome—essentially, looking for a surrogate son. These situations, however, are exceptions. Titillatingly, society wants to point to extremes and to "twisted" or deviant scenarios, but these exceptions have nothing to do with the larger social trend and are not applicable to a difference of just a few years.

Overall, Koberstein has recently seen an anecdotal rise in FAYM relationships, and she notes that it's becoming increasingly socially acceptable. To her, it is an extremely positive trend. When age gaps do not stretch into generational gaps, she says that they can lead to tremendously satisfying, mutual sexual relationships that are fulfilling both physically and emotionally. Their increasing occurrence is simply a natural part of social evolution.

An important thing to note in closing is that none of these factors means that the sexual side of a relationship between a man and woman of the same age or between an older man and a younger woman is less than satisfying. Obviously if this were so, humanity would have halted thousands of years ago. We can all point to successful relationships and marriages between couples in which the man *isn't* younger, but both parties are happy and satisfied with their love lives.

Boiling this all down, FAYM relationships might have a few benefits worth being aware of, but ultimately, they aren't that different from any other kind of relationship. They still include their challenges, and they also contain their moments of beauty.

While many people might still be tempted to gossip and giggle about "the older woman," they'll soon realize that these relationships are only remarkable in that they are so *unremarkable*. As Koberstein puts it, the taboo against women dating younger men is "much ado about nothing." We as a society are finally beginning to see that it's a perfectly natural thing, and in some ways, it can even be a little more fun.

Speaking of fun in FAYM relationships, who can deny that a little extra money to throw around makes a date more fun? In the next chapter, we'll look at the economics of dating younger men. I'll show that it's true that it can be just as much fun to give as to receive.

CHAPTER 7

Her Money, Her Lifestyle

In Chapter 3, we talked about the economic reasons why, in the past, it was preferable and often even necessary for women to date and marry older men. Here's a little secret: Many of those economic arguments can still be made, except that they now can be made in favor of either younger women dating older men or younger men dating older women. A human being—male or female—who is further along in his or her career is very likely to be making more money.

Traditionally, any person doing well in a career had to be a male, and so it was only young women who got to enjoy the perks of dating wealthier beaus who were able to provide them with lifestyles they might not be able to enjoy otherwise.

One of the natural attractions of dating and eventually marrying a well-off man was that he could provide security and even some spoiling. Accordingly, the highest aspiration a female in the '50s could ever hope for arose: marrying a good provider. Her social standing, or even just her ability to have a little fun, could be dramatically changed by her sweetheart's pocketbook.

The more things change, the more they stay the same. Finding the right partner is still a legitimate path to getting a leg up in the world, but it just so happens that in today's world, the partner with the fat pocketbook can just as easily be female as male. One has to realize that men have always received a great deal of pleasure out of being able to "spoil" their girlfriends or wives. It's fun to give gifts of money, clothing, special event tickets, or trips to someone you love. It's also fun to have someone do this for you!

That brings me to yet another benefit of FAYM relationships. The more experienced, established woman can provide her younger husband, boyfriend, or even her casual date with any number of benefits from career mentoring to trendy jeans; any of which he might not have access to at his stage of life and level of income. As it turns out, the role of provider doesn't have to be tied down to one gender. For the same reason, enjoying being provided for is not something that only young women can do.

Imagine a 43 year-old woman named Amanda, a partner in a prominent law firm, who is dating Brian, a 35 year-old man who recently finished his PhD and is looking for an assistant professorship. Amanda is able to take Brian out to dinners regularly that he might otherwise only treat himself to once every couple of months. She has a subscription to a local theater and takes him as her date to every play; without her, even though he is well educated and culturally astute, he would be unlikely even to think about spending money on theater tickets.

She owns a comfortable, professionally decorated, two-bedroom condo, while he rents a room in a bachelor pad with two other grad students. Naturally, they spend most of their time at her place. She has TiVo and automatically stocks her food shelves.

For Brian, dating Amanda is a good deal. First, she's beautiful and in better shape than many women Brian's age. But more importantly, she shares his interests, is extremely intelligent and driven, and has a sexy confidence. On top of that, dating Amanda is a lot of fun for him because she has enough financial freedom to open a broader range of activities to them. If he went the traditional dating route, he might be seeing a 33 year-old woman also caught up in the long, nerve-jangling search for an assistant professorship, or he might be with a 28 year-old who has just taken out yet another $50,000 in student loans to continue her medical school education. Brian would be the more financially independent partner, and so he might only be able to take his date to a movie or dinner at the neighborhood bar and grill. There's nothing wrong with that, but as a rule, it's just more fun to have options.

For Brian and Amanda, the benefits work both ways. It's extremely satisfying and pleasurable to Amanda to feel that she is helping Brian experience things that wouldn't otherwise be within his budget.

If *she* were dating more traditionally, she might be with a 50 year-old broker who also owns a house, subscribes to theatres, and treats himself to fine dining. He'd certainly enjoy Amanda for all she has to offer in terms of charm, intelligence, and personality, but it would be hard for her to feel that she was really able to treat him or introduce him to something new. She might try to surprise him with a gift like a new tie, only to realize weeks later that he never wears it; it's not that he's ungrateful, but he prefers Burberry to the Dior Homme Amanda chose for him. If she gave the same tie to Brian, he'd wear it and wear it proudly.

In many female and younger male relationships, "spoiling" can go far beyond the fancy dates Amanda and Brian enjoy. An established and successful woman is likely to treat herself to vacations in Europe or Caribbean cruises—and if she's in love, or even just in like, she'll certainly want to take her boyfriend with her. Furthermore, she probably surrounds herself with friends who are just as successful as she is. She might be able to spend weekend trips with her boyfriend at her friends' vacation home in a ski area. The couple might enjoy socializing with his friends as well; after all, they're probably well matched in terms of intelligence and career paths. Consequently, she probably has much in common with his friends, too. But odds are his friends aren't yet in a position to invest in property in Newport Beach or Martha's Vineyard.

Perhaps, the younger man is already well on his way to success, and so dating a more established woman doesn't necessarily mean participating in novel experiences but simply doing things in higher style. He might be going to the same concert, but now, he's riding there in a limo and sitting in the front section. He can show up dressed in the designer jeans his older girlfriend bought for him. His girlfriend, in the meantime, has a blast because things are fresh and fun for him. She gains the opportunity to see her lifestyle through his eyes and attend the concert with someone who is excited to be there and wants to stand through the whole thing.

The 50 year-old broker might not approach the experience with the same sense of excitement. As people age and gain more experience, the wonder naturally wears off. Remember the night before a trip to Disneyland when you were a child? It was impossible to sleep. Now, if you go to Disneyland as an adult, you might enjoy it very much, but you'll probably still get a decent night's sleep beforehand. The experience no longer contains the magic of newness.

For a woman, dating a younger man can feel like being the gatekeeper to Disneyland. He's thrilled to ride to the concert in the limo wearing new, hot jeans, and she feels not only the gratification of being the one to provide him with this experience but also the excitement of approaching the experience as if for the first time from his perspective. She'd probably have a very different evening—and go home a lot earlier—if she went with a man ten years her senior.

In addition to the joy of being with a partner excited about things that older men might look at with indifference, boredom, or cynicism, a woman dating a younger man also obtains the added benefit of staying in touch with what's current. The younger people are, the more tapped in they tend to be to current trends in pop culture, communications technology,

music, film, and fashion. For many women, this is a delightful perk.

A woman might be spending a little extra money on those front-row concert seats, but her boyfriend will help her program her new iPod on the way there. If they arrive at the concert, and she realizes, "Well, this is fun, but I've seen this band three times now," then he'll be able to take her to a new indie band concert the next weekend.

In terms of keeping up with the latest trends, women in their thirties and early forties who are dating men in Generation Y (born after 1980) probably get the best deal. With Generation Y, we're starting to see for the first time in decades a generation of young men who care about fashion and style. This was certainly not the case for the Gen-Xers who preceded them. It just didn't take a lot of fashion expertise for a guy to pair a plaid flannel shirt with a pair of grungy jeans and let his hair solidify into a shaggy Kurt Cobain mop.

Men in Generation Y, on the other hand, are label conscious, read *GQ*, and are drawn to personal style that advertises success (or at least refined taste) instead of counterculture ideals. Dating mature women allows them to live out that fantasy and to have access to wardrobes that their post-grad school or first "real job" budgets wouldn't otherwise supply.

Women win in this equation, too. For women, it's

just as much fun to dress a guy as it is to undress him. But in American culture, men in their forties, fifties, and older often aren't interested in fashion. They know how to dress appropriately for the office and usually know not to wear black socks with white tennis shoes, but otherwise, distinguishing one designer label from another is just not a priority for them.If you happen to see a man who's unfortunate enough to find himself out shopping with his girlfriend or wife, he usually looks like he's hoping he'll just die so he won't have to stand there another second. Not so with men in Generation Y! They have the fashion consciousness that pairs perfectly with girlfriends eager to share their eyes for style and their credit cards. The return to fashion among 20-something men is an observable social trend as is the growing acceptability of men dating women who are older than they are.

I'd venture to say that the two trends are so compatible that they're likely to feed each other. Guys dating women who are further ahead financially than they are now have the means to dress in the clothes they covet. More than that—they now have a reason to dress in those clothes because their girlfriends take them to five-star restaurants and hot vacation spots … all the places you just can't show up wearing clothes from a discount store.

If a 30 year-old man plans to spend his weekend at the sports bar with his 30 year-old friends, just about any outfit will do. But if he plans to spend the weekend with his 40 year-old girlfriend and her colleagues in a new condo in wine country, he'll need the right clothes. Most of the time, he's thrilled to have the wardrobe makeover, and she's delighted to play Tim Gunn for a day. It's yet another way that the FAYM relationship satisfies everyone involved.

As women already know, on the other side of the coin, older men are simply less flexible, and they might be inclined to see a woman's attempts to revise their image as encroaching on their power or as criticism. Younger men will be far more interested in and willing to learn from their partners' opinions; this tendency extends into realms of the relationship that bear far more weight than the make of a shoe or the tuck of a shirt.

This is not to say that the woman will automatically dominate all areas of the relationship because the man is younger, but she'll likely enjoy a level of respect from her partner that isn't always a given when the age skew is reversed. Younger men can also stand to gain from their more sophisticated girlfriends in realms beyond the strictly material.

Now that women have made enormous strides in the workforce and hold influential positions as professionals of all kinds, the mentorship they have to offer younger men can be invaluable. Career mentorship has been something that men have offered younger girlfriends and wives for several decades now. Because of their experience and standing in their careers, older men are able to offer younger women just starting out in the same or similar fields access to contacts, recommendations, training, and guidance.

Women have now attained a foothold in business and professional leadership that allows them to extend the same kind of helping hand to their younger boyfriends. The benefits are obvious for men: Dating a woman with important connections is a way to pick up the pace of their career advancements in the same way that in the past young women have been able to help their careers by dating established men. Chances are, too, that at some point in her life the now-older woman dated a man older than herself who offered *her* professional guidance. Now, her younger partner benefits not only from her insights but from the insights of those who previously mentored her. It's like she's part of the good old boys network!

The woman providing mentorship and networking to her younger partner benefits as well. It can be an extremely satisfying experience for her to help someone she likes or loves to get ahead. Her genuine interest in his success and his deep appreciation for her guidance are likely to bring them closer together.

Working together towards a common goal and building something together professionally can be a bonding experience for the couple. This phenomenon has only become possible in recent years not only because it is now increasingly acceptable for women to have younger partners but also because it is now more possible for women to hold high-level positions that allow them to act as mentors in the first place.

Perhaps, the best example I've seen in popular culture of this symbiotic give and take is the relationship between the characters Samantha Jones and Smith Jerrod on *Sex and the City*. When Samantha, a sexually unabashed, successful PR consultant in her forties first meets the significantly younger Smith, she thinks of him as just another sexual partner. But over time, she develops very real feelings for him. When she learns that he is struggling to build an acting career for himself, she flexes her considerable PR muscle to help him. She builds a red carpet event surrounding a play he is starring in (so far off Broadway that it's in Brooklyn), and she gets all the Manhattan literati to attend. She also ensures that his nude, hunky photo is papered all over the city—with one enormous billboard in Times Square—in an ad campaign for Absolut Vodka called Absolut Hunk. Smith becomes an overnight sensation, and his acting career is launched. Even though Smith was smitten with Samantha long before she made him a star, her efforts on his behalf bond the two of them, and their relationship ends up being the closest the commitment-shy Samantha ever comes to settling down.

This story perfectly encapsulates the potential FAYM relationships have for mutual back scratching, which can in turn reveal and bolster deeper feelings of respect, admiration, and partnership. Samantha provides for Smith in a material way by sharpening his image, and she offers invaluable support that moves his career forward with a speed that he simply couldn't have achieved on his own.

But these favors aren't solely offered and accepted in the name of material gain. Instead, they are the natural next step for a couple in which each partner has something to offer the other, and the exchange allows the relationship to grow as a whole. FAYM relationships throw the door wide open for this kind of collaboration and mutual growth.

Some women might wonder, "Okay, maybe it's a good thing for my guy to be bright-eyed and eager to learn . . . but isn't there going to be a little immaturity that goes along with that?" It's a fair question, and in the next chapter, we'll explore the pop culture wisdom that men are less mature than women are. Is there any truth to it? Should it have any bearing on the age range of men that women are willing to date?

CHAPTER 8

"But He's Too Immature!"

"**I**'m raising three children: my son, my daughter, and my husband."

It's a common joke among busy wives and mothers, and a scenario most Americans can easily picture. In a marriage, the job of picking up a man's dirty socks and ensuring he remembers his thermos of coffee on his way out the door often falls to his wife. She ends up filling a role for him that is in many ways similar to the role she fills for her children: She mothers him. Most of the time, we can all share an easy-going chuckle over the joke because these gender roles are all too familiar.

At the same time, that joke stems from the fact that many Americans tend to take for granted the folk wisdom that men, as a group, are less mature than women are. In any conversation about whether it's appropriate for women to date younger men, this topic is bound to come up. Men's maturity, or lack of it, is one of the top reasons women cite for not wanting to date younger men. They look for men who are a few years older because they argue that men need a head start of several years to rise to an acceptable level of maturity.

But what exactly do they mean when they talk about "maturity" as it applies to the differences between the sexes? In this chapter I will take a closer look at the very complex concept of maturity and show that, actually, it's much less relevant than we may think when it comes to FAYM relationships.

Most of the time, when people talk about maturity, they're really referring to responsibility. For example, when we see a young person juggling school, a few extracurricular activities, and a part-time job and doing well with all of them, we tend to say, "Wow, he's very mature for his age." But what we really mean is that he has a strong sense of responsibility.

On the other hand, if we have a friend who rarely returns phone calls, can never find his keys, and tends to show up late most of the time, we likely shrug our shoulders and say, "Fred is so immature." But Fred might be a 40 year-old man. What's more accurate and more *specific* is to say that he isn't particularly responsible. Fred might be in his sixties and still be irresponsible. Maybe that's why he's still available!

In the dating world, responsibility is often high on women's lists of must-have traits in potential partners, but that's not always a given. As more and more people date just for fun rather than as a step toward marriage, it's harder to generalize what makes a dating partner desirable. The guidelines are a lot looser when you're deciding who would be fun to have dinner with instead of who would make a good husband and father.

In fact, I have an aunt who decided to divorce my uncle because he was a little *too* dependable. She wanted to date someone who would be fun, wild, unpredictable, and . . . well, not quite so *responsible*. So, it's important to remember that we no longer live in a dating climate where it's possible to define a set standard for the most eligible bachelor. One woman's "no, thank you" is another woman's hot date.

When it comes to long-term relationships, in general, women prefer to date responsible men—men who accomplish the things they are expected to complete at home and at work, can be relied on to call when they say they will, and are willing to be held accountable for their actions, good and bad. Often, women automatically associate a strong sense of responsibility with age, and they worry that if they choose to date a younger man, they'll end up with someone who can't take care of himself.

More often than not, however, responsibility is a trait that you can see in people, male and female, from a very young age, and it doesn't necessarily change much over time. The child who forgets his homework at age eight will often become the man who misses deadlines at age 48, and the child who helps his mother with the dishes at age seven will often become the man who willingly takes on half of the housework at age 47. Some people are responsible; some are not; and they tend to stay that way!

When a woman says that she wants a mature man but means she wants a *responsible* one, she'd be much better off looking closely at her partner's personal characteristics than at the date on his birth certificate.

Women also tend to use the word "maturity" to describe a man's interest in being part of a committed, monogamous relationship. As with responsibility, men's willingness to commit has much more to do with individual personality than with age.

Whether they're 20, 30, or 60, some men prefer to date for fun, and some men date because they're seeking long-term relationships. I certainly know of several young men who were ready to marry right out of college; at 21, they wanted commitment in their lives.

As a group, however, it seems that young men don't start to think about marriage as early as young women do. It's entirely possible that this is a cultural phenomenon that has simply lingered since the days when men had to postpone marriage because they were the sole breadwinners. Now that women also possess the option of postponing marriage and family in favor of education and career, we're starting to see them more in line with men in terms of marrying later in life.

Largely due to the Women's Movement, men and women now enjoy a period in their twenties that is much more about personal exploration and growth than about laying the foundations for a family. They attend college and even graduate or professional school; then, they establish themselves in a career.

Therefore, if "maturity" means willingness to commit, it might well be true that men in their early to mid-twenties do not necessarily race towards the altar *en masse*. But the new reality of our culture is that the same holds true for women in their early to mid-twenties. Beyond that age, as with responsibility, willingness to commit depends much more on the individual than on age.

Consequently, when women say, "He's too immature" but mean "responsible" or "willing to commit," we realize that, ultimately, it turns out that neither of those qualities is hitched to the age wagon.

A third thing they might actually be referring to when they talk about "maturity" is an adult way of behaving, or in other words, when women accuse men of being "immature," they might really mean that they have bad manners and are not willing to do things that don't offer instant gratification or that require unselfishness.

Overall, it would be difficult to argue that men as a group are more immature than women. However, it is possible that some differences between the sexes are labeled "immaturity" but are really more about personality.

For example, a woman may label a man immature because he still likes video games, cartoons, and making funny faces; however, this childlikeness can be charming to women rather than obnoxious because it appeals to their instinct to nurture.

Of course, exceptions always exist to any general rule about human nature, but for the most part, women are both biologically predisposed and culturally encouraged to be nurturing.

Often, women don't mind taking care of the family in more traditional ways, such as making dinner or maintaining a nice home; it's a source of pride and appeals to their mothering instincts. When a partner's personality complements a woman's tendency to nurture, it might be that what we've become accustomed to calling "immaturity" is actually a positive thing for the relationship.

For example, a woman can find it charming when the kids get out their tee-ball set, and Daddy wants to play too. Or it can be endearing to another woman that while she reads *The Brothers Karamazov* on the subway to work, her boyfriend plays Super Monkey Ball on his iPhone and proudly announces his high score.

Some adult men still absentmindedly play with their food when no one is watching. They burrow little tunnels in their mashed potatoes or draw faces on their pancakes with syrup. If a woman catches her boyfriend doing that in the privacy of their own home, she's usually more likely to think, "Look what simple things make him happy" than to be disgusted.

As another example, my husband still loves to have chicken tenders with chocolate milk. It's kids' food, and I find it heartwarming that it's still his favorite thing to eat. Some 40 year-old men love to wrestle and goof off, and they're always a big hit with the children at the family reunion. Most grown men play video games just as avidly as high school kids do. In fact, according to the Pew Research Center, about a third of adult men in the United States play video games on gaming consoles compared to only about a fifth of women.

A less technologically sophisticated example is the dad who walks into the living room, finds his kid's toy car on the floor, and starts zooming it across the rug into the wall and saying, "Pow!" If his wife walked into the living room and found the same toy car lying around, she'd probably pick it up and put it away, but if she happened to walk in while he was playing with the car, she'd probably smile.

Have you ever noticed that when a guy has a cold—whether he's 8 or 48—the world grinds to a halt? He needs a woman to bring him something warm to drink, rub Vicks on his chest, and tell him how sorry she is that he has a stuffy nose. If, on the other hand, a grown woman gets a cold, she takes a DayQuil, and the world keeps on turning.

Of course, there's the classic example of the guy who likes to sneak up behind his girlfriend and tickle her or pick her up. It may indeed be the same way he related to girls in junior high, but it still works for him now because his ability to let go and goof around charms women. It might be easy to accuse a 25 year-old man of immaturity when he likes to put a dorky hat on sideways and laugh with his buddies about how silly he looks, but chances are that he'll be just as willing to do the same thing at age 55.

At this point, you have to wonder what it actually means when a woman says, "I can't date younger men because they're too immature." Does it count when it's a 35 year-old woman talking about dating a 32 year-old man? For that matter, what about a 55 year-old woman talking about dating a 52 year-old man? If she followed today's cultural pressures, she'd have to reject that 52 year-old and find a 58 year-old. Really, when it comes to maturity, can we say there's any difference between a man of 52 and a man of 58? When women use the phrase "too immature," they might actually mean a number of other things. But the fact remains that age is almost never the true factor in her complaint.

If age is not a likely predictor when it comes to facets of maturity like responsibility, willingness to commit, and childlikeness, there is one area where it's safe to bet that younger men will be *more* "mature," so to speak, than older men. That's the subject of a mini-chapter, as it's important enough to be discussed on its own.

CHAPTER 9

True Equality

Imagine a 40 year-old woman named Molly out on the dating scene. She's been seeing Nate, who's 34, and Craig, who's 46. In both cases, there's a six-year age difference, but Molly would say that both Nate and Craig are pretty much on the same level in terms of responsibility and desire to start a long-term relationship with the right woman. However, Molly notices one area caused by the difference between Nate and Craig's ages—or rather the age in which they grew up.

The reality is that the Women's Movement occurred not that long ago, and on occasion, Molly can see that while Craig grew up in a time when women were still second-class citizens, Nate came of age in a time when women and men were peers. Craig's parents met in the 1950s, while Nate's parents met in the 1970s. The Women's Movement happened in between those two decades, and this causes the difference between Craig and Nate.

While Craig's parents began their family in the '60s with the old, traditional roles, Nate's parents began their family in the midst of the Women's Movement. Every now and then, Craig's attitude reveals a psychology fostered by inequality. His mother went to college but never worked outside the home, and the same was true for most of his friends' mothers. On the other hand, Nate's mother was a lawyer, and she actually made slightly more money than his father did.

Living in such different periods influenced both men. Craig was raised in a world in which women were certainly respected but not seen as equals. Nate takes for granted that Molly is a person, just like him. As it turns out, the 12 years between Craig and Nate make a huge difference in their ability truly to accept women's equality. Ultimately, Molly chooses to start a relationship with Nate because in dating someone

younger, she gains a man who sees her the same way she sees herself.

Nate naturally grew up thinking, "Of course, my sister is a real person; of course, I can be friends with girls and guys." When he talked with his friends about their college major, whether grad school was in the picture, or what they wanted to accomplish with their lives, his female friends were included in the conversation without exception and without anyone even remarking that it was special or unusual. It never struck Nate as strange, cute, or impressive that his female friends might become attorneys, doctors, or CEOs; he viewed them the same way he did his male friends.

When Craig was growing up, the only female character on the deck of *Star Trek* was Lieutenant Uhura, the "Communications Officer"—a glorified receptionist. In contrast, Nate watched *Star Trek: Voyager* with Captain *Kathryn* Janeway heading the ship. Today, as a grown man, he looks at women as complete people rather than partial people. Naturally, Molly finds that she has much more in common psychologically with Nate than with Craig.

This acceptance of women as whole people will be more common among younger men than older men. Because the Women's Movement was such a long time coming and developed incrementally, the younger a man is, the more likely he will not only have accepted the idea of equality intellectually but will have experienced it growing up and even assimilated it into his psychology.

Even if a woman is 50, she doesn't necessarily have to look for a 34 year-old Nate to find a man who can be respectful of her, but she will be more likely to find him in, for example, a 42 year-old than in a 58 year-old. The younger a man is, the more cultural influences will have shaped his psychology and so the more likely he'll be to be able to have a mutually respectful relationship with a woman.

Even in those areas where a certain way of behaving is, in general, "a guy thing," younger men still don't deserve a bad rap. It turns out that, sure, they might like to goof off or to be cared for, but so do men of all ages. At the same time, younger men come with the added benefit of honoring equality more. The younger they are, the more likely they are to view women as women view themselves. That certainly is a strong factor in compatibility.

When seeking a long-term partner who will understand her, a woman is more likely to find it happening naturally with a younger man. And even if she is just planning a movie date, it is more likely she and the man will view the characters in the same light if the man considers women his equal. In this realm, the younger man is the more mature man.

As long as we're on the topic of maturity, what do

FAYM relationships look like in the "mature" years as couples grow old together? Do FAYM relationships that begin when both partners are relatively young fare well as the pair grows older? What about FAYM relationships that begin when both partners are older—after a divorce or after the death of a first spouse? We'll look at this in the next chapter on FAYM relationships in the senior years.

CHAPTER 10

Growing Old Together

What does the FAYM relationship look like in the senior years? We must actually ask two separate questions. First, do FAYM relationships work when they begin late in life—say, a 72 year-old woman dating a 68 year-old man? Second, do FAYM relationships that begin earlier in life last as the couple approaches retirement age?

Let's look at the question of dating later in life

first. What benefits exist for senior-age singles who choose FAYM relationships? AARP, the mainstay of the retired American population, recently surveyed singles aged 40 to 69 about their romantic lives. The survey found that only about one in ten of these singles had no interest in dating whatsoever. The remaining 90 percent were all invested in romance in some way; 31 percent were in an exclusive dating relationship; 32 percent dated non-exclusively; 13 percent were not dating but were actively looking for dates, and 14 percent would be interested in dating if the right person happened to come along.

The picture is clear: The dating scene in America has shifted dramatically. We used to think of dating as the terrain of the 20-somethings. It was strictly for young, childless men, and women seeking marriage for the first time. For those unfortunates who found themselves single again in their forties and beyond, whether due to the death of a spouse or to divorce— tough luck. The idea of an older man or woman hitting the dating scene was just a little strange.

Today, the profile of a typical dater is much different. Men and women who have already been married once (or more than once), have adult children, and are well-established in their careers or already retired make up a larger portion of the dating community than green-behind-the-ears 20 year-olds.

Dating is no longer a rite of passage young people

go through on the road to securing a spouse. Marriage is no longer necessarily the goal or the point. People date casually; they date as a pastime; they date to make friends.

Older Americans who have "been there, done that" in the marriage department discover that just because they aren't necessarily eager to walk down the aisle again doesn't mean they're doomed to live their remaining decades—which might be quite a few—in lonely celibacy. People realize that they feel as vital in their sixties and beyond as they did in their forties, so why shut the blinds and go to bed at 7 PM? They are capable of enjoying—and need—companionship and a physical relationship as much as any other adult. Sixty really is the new 40.

That situation makes dating an older American's game just as much as it is a younger person's game. But here's the hard irony for older American women: In the past, as they aged, their pool of potential candidates decreased. In the United States, women tend to outlive men by a little over five years. It's a sad reality, but any American who has visited a retirement community or long-term care facility is well aware of this fact. There are simply more older women than older men. When you consider the number of older *single* women versus older single men, the odds become even bleaker.

In general, women in the currently retired generations are often married to men older than them-selves. Since women statistically tend to outlive men, this cultural practice can add up to an enormous gap of time between a husband's death and a wife's death. Consider Elizabeth, a 63 year-old woman whose husband passed away several years ago at age 70. Elizabeth mourned for her husband Rick for several years; they had been married nearly 40 years, and his death after a battle with cancer was a heartbreaking experience for her.

But recently, Elizabeth has begun to feel like her old self. She is healthy and fit and has every reason to look forward to several more decades of active life. Her daughter Jennifer has started to drop little hints to Elizabeth about how much fun it would be for her to find a beau. Elizabeth knows Jennifer's right. She's not exactly pining with loneliness, but she has many activities in her life—from golfing to a regular film club. She's the kind of woman who loves people and would prefer to do things with someone rather than by herself.

Elizabeth decides to start making baby steps to-wards dating again. But when she looks around for new dating partners, she quickly finds that she's sur-rounded by widowed female acquaintances but has very few widower acquaintances. Most of the men in her circle are married, and their wives are, for the most part, younger and healthier than their husbands.

She knows a few lifelong bachelors, but she has her doubts about whether they'd make good partners after so many years of independence. That's when Jennifer says, "Wake up, Mom! You're looking at the 70 year-old men! What about men closer to your age—like 58 year-olds?"

In Chapter 4, we discussed how the sexuality patterns of men and women over the course of a lifetime can actually be more in sync when the female partner is older. My point in this chapter is quite similar. Of course, perks and drawbacks occur in every relationship, and it's impossible to point to one fixed kind of coupledom as the ideal that will guarantee success.

However, for the same reason, it's equally impossible to guarantee a couple's failure based on arbitrary social taboos. I'm not making the argument that a FAYM relationship is *better* than any other relationship—merely that it's another possibility, yet another way to expand the pool of possible candidates.

Even though it's a type of relationship that has been relegated to the margins of society for so long, people simply haven't had the opportunity to consider before the many benefits of the FAYM relationship. One of those benefits is that growing older together and having more time together at the end of life is more likely when the female partner is older. As with the scientific reality that lifetime sexual cycles are more in sync when the woman is older, life expectancy tends to overlap more equally in FAYM relationships.

This benefit applies in both scenarios that I described at the beginning of this chapter. It affects FAYM couples that met and married earlier in life; and it affects all couples as they grow older. FAYM couples have the possibility of spending more years together because the man is statistically less likely to pass away before his wife. In Elizabeth's case, and others like her, it applies to women who become single again later in life and discover that they have much higher chances of finding datable men if they consider younger as well as older men.

In either situation, the result might be a couple in which the man is 58, and the woman is 63. Of course, it's impossible to make predictions about what the future might hold for every couple, but statistically, this couple possesses a significantly higher chance of experiencing the twilight of life together rather than one partner being left to face years, or even decades, alone.

Anyone who has watched his or her parents, older friends, or relatives deal with the death of a spouse or long-term partner knows that losing a partner of many years is one of the most difficult parts of growing old. The AARP survey results reinforce this idea when the survey asked, "What is the worst part of being single?" In response, 41 percent of older singles

chose "not having someone around with whom to do things." Eighteen percent chose "nobody around to take care of me when I am sick, disabled, or need help," and another 21 percent chose "fear of being alone in the future." Older people who lose their partners face not only the pain of grief but also the fear or simple loneliness of being without a partner, which can be all the more difficult for those who have been attached for many, many years. Overcoming the taboo against FAYM relationships is just one more way of coping with this difficult stage of life. Women will gain more options beyond spending the last years of their lives alone.

Because of the increase in the FAYM relationship, particularly those now in their twenties, thirties and forties, American society will eventually reach a place 30 or 40 years down the road where the image of retirement homes populated only by widowed women will become a less painfully familiar cliché.

At the same time, women now in their fifties, sixties, and seventies who are single or newly single will also begin to open themselves to the possibility of younger men as well as older men, where the pickings are slimmer. Simply, more men will be available in their fifties to mid-seventies than in their mid-seventies to eighties, and so we will begin to see an increasing number of single women in their seventies and beyond dating younger men.

Increasingly, people will realize that this is sensible. The older a person is, the less a gap of a few years matters in terms of life stages. For example, a 25 year-old woman dating a 20 year-old man deals with an age gap that represents fully 20 percent of her life. In terms of life experience and ability to relate to one another, this could ultimately prove to be a large hurdle for the relationship.

Now compare that scenario to Lucinda, one of Elizabeth's good friends. Lucinda is 70 and dating a 65 year-old man named Drew. The age gap between them represents only 7 percent of Lucinda's life. The differences between her life experiences and Drew's are negligible. There's simply no reason in her case to suggest that Drew might be a less viable option. In terms of experience, perspective, and successfulness, it's unlikely that he'll have anything less to offer than a 75 year-old man will.

In many ways, Lucinda's relationship with Drew might have fewer stresses than a relationship she might have with a 75 year-old. Often, at the end of life, when one partner suffers a stroke or a debilitating disease like Alzheimer's or advanced diabetes, it is the healthy partner who assumes the caretaker role. The healthy partner is often the woman—particularly, when she's younger. Ironically, she's also often the physically smaller of the two, but she is left to do the literal heavy lifting. Helping a spouse bathe, use the bathroom, get in and out of bed, or up and down the stairs can be very hard on anyone and is particularly difficult for women who are smaller than the ailing husbands for which they are caring.

There's also the emotional stress. In fact, studies have found that caring for a partner with a debilitating illness can be so physically, emotionally, and spiritually draining that caretakers, statistically, die first. If a woman's partner is younger than she is by a few years, the odds decrease that the burden of caretaking will fall to her. She and her partner will more likely be on equal footing in terms of physical health. Even if the burden of caretaking is not an issue in the relationship, a senior woman will gain other benefits when her partner is younger.

An old joke that I love involves two women in their seventies chatting; one says to the other, "I hear you're marrying Mr. Pierce."

"That's right," her friend answers.

"He's not a nice man," the first woman says frankly.

"No, he isn't," her friend agrees.

"He's not very handsome."

"No."

"He doesn't have any money."

"No."

"So, why on earth are you marrying him?"

"Because he can drive at night."

There's some truth to the joke. A woman in her seventies who's still energetic and eager to enjoy her retirement shouldn't feel constrained by social mores to only date men in their eighties who might not be interested in the same activities she is or even able to keep up with her. She might enjoy having a travel partner or even a tennis partner, for that matter. She might enjoy having someone to take her to dinner and dancing. Energetically, she'll be much better matched with a man who is slightly younger than with an older man.

Her younger partner won't necessarily be sacrificing anything either. Women who are in their seventies today grew up in a culture with increasing awareness of nutrition and exercise. Oftentimes, they have the means, knowledge, and desire to be fit and active much later in life than was ever thought possible in the past. If 60 is the new 40, then 80 is the new 60. There's no reason why a 70 year-old man wouldn't consider himself lucky to catch many of these women at 74. It's not as though their physiques would be much different.

A woman may also discover psychological benefits of dating a younger man later in life. In the previous chapter, we saw that younger men tend to have absorbed the psychology of equality between the sexes more than older men. They are more able to see women in the way that women see themselves.

This dynamic is particularly true for generations who are of retirement age today. They lived through the cusp of the Women's Movement. Perhaps, when they were some of the first to be graduating from college, it was still unusual for women to have career ambitions. Over the course of their lifetime, they saw major shifts in society's attitudes towards women. They lived through the period when opportunities for women in the professional sphere expanded well beyond being a secretary or a teacher.

An age difference of ten years could represent huge changes in perspective for people in these generations. For example, before she met Drew, Lucinda went out a few times with an 80 year-old man named Steven. Steven was born in 1929 and lived his entire life surrounded by women who fulfilled very traditional roles—who stayed home, maintained a household, raised children, and were barred from an education and a career.

Drew, on the other hand, was in his twenties when women marched for equality in the 1970s. He witnessed social change in a very close and personal way in the lives of all his female peers. He also watched his son grow up to be a very different husband and father than he was. All around him, he now sees men only a few years younger than himself assuming an equal share of the responsibilities of family and home. It wasn't a mammoth logical leap for Drew to realize,

"Gee, maybe it wasn't exactly fair for me to leave all the cooking, cleaning, and childrearing to my wife in my first marriage." When Drew met Lucinda, he was—at the ripe age of 65—more prepared to be an equal participant in the relationship. He assumed a new attitude and was more willing to take on responsibilities that he might automatically have relegated to Lucinda in the past. Steven, on the other hand, wasn't able to make this psychological shift . . . so it's no small wonder that Lucinda didn't continue her relationship with him and chose Drew instead.

Certainly, if both partners are retired, there's no reason why they both can't participate equally, which would take some of the burden off the woman so that she can enjoy her retirement as much as her partner enjoys his. Like Lucinda and Drew, older FAYM couples can make a very compatible team in that way.

Again, the younger the man is, the greater the chances are that he will have not only accepted but truly begun to incorporate the changes brought on by the Women's Movement. He is more likely to be a better psychological match for a woman.

Often, the psychological benefits of dating a younger man later in life relate not only to gender differences but also to generational differences. When Lucinda chose between Steven and Drew, she was essentially choosing between the Silent Generation and the Baby Boomer Generation. Of

course, it's impossible to make sweeping generalizations about people in any group, but there are certainly some identifiable and significant differences in the collective mindsets of these two generations.

In general, members of the Silent Generation grew up in a time when the Depression and World War II had dampened Americans' spirits. To get by, they learned to keep their heads down, to work hard, not to question authority, and to limit their expectations.

In contrast, the Baby Boomers came of age during the '60s and '70s, and their generation tends to be defined by the open attitudes of the Peace Movement, the Civil Rights Movement, and the Women's Movement. This generation values standing up for oneself and taking risks to achieve goals. Baby Boomers might be more likely than members of the Silent Generation to be a little more creative in their lives and with problem solving.

Both the younger generation and the older one have their strengths and weaknesses. But it's possible that a Baby Boomer might be more fun in a dating context—particularly for a retired woman who is no longer attaching goals like marriage and family to her romantic relationships. If the idea is just to share the freedom of retirement with a fun partner, the Baby Boomer's way of life fits the bill.

Look at, for example, Andy Williams or Perry

Como in their sixties versus Mick Jagger, Harrison Ford, and Rick Springfield (singer of "Jessie's Girl") in *their* sixties. Baby Boomers simply aren't accepting old age gracefully; as long as their bodies and minds will allow them to, they want to continue living like exuberant children. As their own kids grow up and leave the house, they don't say, "Good, now I have some time to relax and look at the photo albums." They say, "Good, now I can start playing hard again."

Although there is no way to predict any individual's ongoing health, one thing is certain: Women who are currently at or beyond retirement age grew up in a time when it was unusual and even undesirable to date younger men. But today, the reasons that fostered this taboo have receded.

There is no reason, then, for women to limit themselves to the shrinking pool of candidates who are older than they are. They have a good chance of finding a compatible, energetic, healthy partner among men who are younger; so why impose arbitrary limits? Both partners only stand to gain in terms of more equal life expectancy, better-matched lifestyles and energy levels, and more compatible attitudes towards women's place in society.

In addition, women in their twenties, thirties, and forties looking for a lasting, lifelong relationship can now consider a FAYM relationship for the same reasons. If they are forward thinking, they'll realize that a younger man is the best bet in terms of a partnership that will last a lifetime.

We've now dealt with one of the biggest reasons why people couple up in the first place: having a partner with whom to face the twilight of life. But what about the other big reason—having a partner with whom to face the *dawning* of life? That's right—making babies. Are FAYM relationships well suited for parenting? Is there any chance that a woman's age might prove an obstacle? Read on to find out.

CHAPTER 11

Making Babies the FAYM Way

Chapter 3 touched on the fact that the practice of women only dating and marrying older men has very strong cultural, economic, and biological roots. One of the most important of these was the fact that in the past, younger women had the best chance—and often the *only* chance—of getting pregnant and giving birth to healthy babies. Men who wanted to start families could usually do so at just about any adult age but only if they chose wives in their teens or twenties.

Women in their thirties were simply considered to be beyond their childbearing years. Naturally, this biological reality reinforced the pressure for men to choose younger women and for women to marry young. The fear surrounding the expiration date on female fertility was so strong that even today it remains a huge cause of couples' anxieties.

One of the first things that both men and women wonder when FAYM relationships are introduced is "Would it change the options for having children?" The answer is, overwhelmingly, *not a bit*.

Biological and economic considerations in family planning have changed so drastically in the last quarter century that we just can't rely on the old cultural model anymore to tell us the "perfect" way to build our families.

Let's look at the economic side of the equation first. Centuries and even decades ago, young men were expected to obtain an education, find a job, then build up some financial security, and finally, marry and start a family. A young man's sense of self-worth, accomplishment, and pride hinged on his ability to support his wife and children.

Society encouraged young women, on the other hand, to take on the roles of a wife and mother. Their sense of self-worth and accomplishment came not

from career strides but from their ability to rear and nurture a happy, healthy family. It only made sense, then, for men to start families later in life—when they could be the best providers possible—and for women to start families earlier in life—when they were at the height of their fertility.

Today, however, it's just as likely for a woman to seek fulfillment and accomplishment in a career as it is for a man. To a greater extent than ever before, society recognizes and values women's contributions in the workplace. As a result, today's young women apply to law school or launch businesses with the same motivation and drive that their grandmothers channeled into homemaking.

So, if both men and women in their twenties are focusing on a career, when does the family planning start? It starts later—for both sexes.

Fortunately, advancements in science have kept pace with advancements in equality. Since the first successful in vitro fertilization was performed in the late 1970s, fertility medicine has advanced rapidly. Even in the 1980s, women had many doubts about having a baby beyond the age of 30. Today, giving birth after 30 is almost a given. People now tend to think of the childbearing years as lasting until about age 45. In fact, in certain social spheres, it's very unusual to have a baby in one's twenties.

In the years since no-fault divorce, society's expectations of marriage have evolved, and young people now approach the prospect of marrying and starting a family very cautiously. They want to make sure that the fit is just right; if it's not, they're not going to make the gamble.

First, they date extensively, then cohabitate, then marry; even then, they spend time as a couple traveling together and enjoying the company of other young, childless couples. It's not until their early to mid-thirties that children begin to enter the discussion. It's simply a new lifestyle preference. If you add ambitious career goals to the mix, it's easy to see that today's young people often just don't have time for babies in their twenties.

In the meantime, increasingly, women are having babies in their late thirties and forties. In the United States in 2005, 111,000 women over 40 gave birth—the highest number of births over 40 ever. In Great Britain, the number of women over 40 who gave birth doubled between 1990 and 2000. As science continues to shed light on fertility, we can only assume that the number will continue to increase.

Evidently, we're entering a new social era, and it's time we revised our image of "typical" motherhood. It's no longer just a 20-something woman's game. Consequently, men interested in starting a family suddenly find themselves with expanding options.

In the past, if a man fell in love with a woman

in her thirties, he risked foregoing children. It was much more prudent for a 33 year-old, family-minded bachelor to date 20-something women than it was to date women his own age or older.

Today, however, the 33 year-old bachelor can double his chances of finding a woman with which he'd like to raise a family. Sure, he can date women in their twenties, but now he can also date women in their thirties—without any fear of compromising his hopes for having children.

Of course, modern medicine can't trump biology entirely. Doctors still agree that beyond 40, the risks of pregnancy and childbirth increase significantly for a woman and her child. Beyond 45, pregnancies are rare. I'm not suggesting that age is no longer a factor at all.

But here come the celebrities again; as noted in a *Los Angeles Times'* article entitled "California's risky trend: an over-40 baby boom," which appeared in December of 2007, a study from the Public Policy Institute of California showed that although only 5 percent of all California births were from women age 40 to 44, that number increased by 300 percent between 1982 and 2007. Since several of these new older moms are celebrities, including *Desperate Housewives* star Marcia Cross, Holly Hunter, and Geena Davis, the Times article notes that they "made it look easy." The article did discuss the increased risks for women in their forties, but clearly, many women do have children at this age.

In addition, according to the State of California's Department of Finance Report, of the 566,137 births in 2007 in California, 5 percent or more than 27,800 births were to women between the ages of 40 and 44. The same report projects that in terms of age-specific fertility rates, the birth rates for women ages 40 to 44 will increase by 18.6 percent between 2008 and 2018.

The point? Once again, I am not passing moral judgment, and I certainly am not in the least bit qualified to provide health advice for older mothers. However, medical advancements that allow women to bear children through their thirties have created more balance in the ideal parenting ages of men and women.

Nevertheless, giving birth and raising a child is not the same thing. Raising a baby is, obviously, not strictly a matter of biological capability. We must also be mindful of those little issues of care and nurturing, but we now live in a society where fathers are as equally responsible for childrearing as mothers are. Rising in the middle of the night to feed a crying baby, chasing an excited toddler around the backyard, teaching a child to ride a bike, setting and keeping a curfew for a teenager eager to test the limits—all of those daily parenting demands drain enormous energy reserves.

In the past, men could father children at just about any age and then turn over the daily mental and physical requirements of childrearing to their young and energetic wives. Now that men are becoming as equally invested in the minutiae of childrearing as women, it's no longer quite so appealing for men to delay having children past a certain age. All of this means that in today's society, there's a period of a couple decades when it's ideal for both men and women to have children—partly because of biological influences *and* because, well, kids take energy. However, if the woman is a bit older, she'll likely have a higher salary and be more able to hire a nanny (or at least a maid) to help with some of the work and to conserve some of the parents' energy.

Yes, it is true: Biologically speaking, a FAYM relationship might not be the best pairing for having biological children if a woman is in her mid-forties or beyond. However, increasingly, as our society's conception of parenting evolves, a man might not want to have his first child much beyond the age of 40 either.

In addition, most men who have chosen to remain bachelors into their forties are not necessarily seeking a dating or married relationship with the goal of children. As they say, "If it hasn't happened yet, it's never gonna happen." But for those few 40 and over men who *are* interested in having children for the first time, the good news is that non-traditional, blended families are much more likely and possible beyond age 40.

For a man considering a child at age 32, if he is dating or marrying a woman who is 36, his ability to have children is certainly a biological possibility. If a man in his early forties falls in love with a slightly older woman for whom biological children are no longer a possibility, she will often be bringing children into the relationship from a previous marriage. Her new husband would then have the opportunity to act as a father figure to his stepchildren. Alternatively, a FAYM couple could choose to adopt. Adoption agencies will likely see their extra years—that imply maturity and financial security—as a plus.

Ultimately, the key point remains that only a small window of years exists when a woman's age-related infertility and a man's continued desire to have children might overlap and conflict in a FAYM relationship. In addition, if a couple *does* fall within that window, there's more than one way to start a family. It's clear that no insurmountable drawbacks exist in a FAYM relationship for men who want to start families, but even more excitingly, women who want children gain some significant benefits in these relationships.

Look at it this way. Say a 35 year-old woman named Erin decides she's ready to marry and have children. She could travel the traditional route and look for a partner who's her age or up to ten years older. *Alternatively*, I'm arguing she could add potential partners who are up to ten years younger than she is. Suddenly she's dating men anywhere from 25 to 45 years old. That's a 20-year span. She's almost certainly going to find that those 20 years make a huge difference, particularly when it comes to the possibility of raising children.

Objectively, by adding men aged from 25 to 35 to her pool of potential candidates, Erin doubles her chances of finding a partner. Before she had only men aged 35 to 45 to date, now she still has them plus the younger set. The pool increases twofold.

But that's just the sheer numbers game. If we then examine the likelihood that the men Erin's dating will want to become fathers, we'll find that her chances of finding a partner actually triple or even quadruple. Why? Logically, men in the younger group will generally be more interested in starting families than the men in the older group. They find themselves at the more typical age for starting families; they're more energetic and less likely to have children from a previous marriage. They won't have the time demands—not to mention the emotional demands—of raising other children on the weekends.

Even if Erin dates an older man who hasn't been married before and doesn't have children, he'll come with his own set of issues. Her girlfriends will want to know, "Well, why is he 45 and never married? Does he have commitment issues?" Let's face it: Likely, they'll be right; at the least, an older man will be more set in his ways than a younger man. To him, having a girlfriend or a wife might be fun, but what about adding children to his life? He might feel he just doesn't want to make that kind of adjustment. The questions of getting married and the question of having children will be completely separate negotiations in his book.

The younger men that Erin dates would simply be able to enter a relationship with less baggage, which will make the prospect of starting a family much simpler and more appealing for Erin *and* her new partner. This brings me to the most surprising part of the conversation. Starting a family with a younger man isn't just easier psychologically. It's easier biologically!

That's right: Men's fertility has an expiration date too.

A recent study at Soroka University in Israel found that men's semen quantity is highest between the ages of 30 and 35 and that it only goes downhill thereafter. The study also found that men over 55 had 54 percent fewer sperm that were "strong swimmers" than men between the ages of 30 and 35.

Another study, conducted at the Lawrence Livermore National Laboratory and the University of

California at Berkeley, found that the older men are, the more likely it is that their sperm carries genetic defects.

Consequently, older men will not only be less able to create a pregnancy, but also they are less likely to create healthy children free of certain birth defects. Further, the older a man is, the less likely it is that his sperm will be successful in an in-vitro fertilization procedure. A study at the Assuta Medical Center in Israel found a possible link between IVF failure and male age. All eggs used in the study came from female donors of a specific age group, so the women's age could be ruled out as a contributing factor. Ultimately, the scientists concluded that the sperm of men over 40 decreased in quality, possibly leading to the failure of IVF procedures.

Yikes, right? At 35, Erin already feels a little nervous about her own fertility. She's eager to find a partner, but she doesn't want to settle on just any guy. Why shouldn't she dramatically increase her chances of finding a partner by looking among younger men? Not only will she double the number of men who might be her soul mate and triple or quadruple her chances of finding a man who's just as interested in having children as she is, but she'll also be radically increasing her chances of actually getting pregnant. If she does need IVF (which is a possibility, since she's over 35), she'll have a better chance of success with a younger man. Given the choice, any woman would sooner gamble on young, Olympian sperm than retired sperm that does a few laps at the Y a couple times a week. In addition, with a man who is her age or younger, she actually increases her odds of having a genetically healthier baby.

I realize that I risk making myself unpopular with men over 40; exceptions to every scientific generalization exist, and any man over 40 reading this probably already knows he is the exception. All joking aside, I'm not arguing that all couples composed of younger women and older men aren't good candidates for becoming biological parents. Obviously, this kind of pairing has worked for centuries and will continue to work.

However, I do want both men and women to recognize that just because it has been the norm in the past for women to be younger than their partners doesn't automatically mean that's the ideal— or only—way to go. Over the course of this book, we've learned there's simply no reason why a woman should feel ashamed of being in a loving relationship with a younger man. Likewise, no reason exists why a woman should feel ashamed of being a few years younger than her boyfriend or husband or of having the same birth date.

As it turns out, many people might not have considered the various pluses to FAYM relationships because of cultural stigma—especially when it comes to a couple's odds of having children. In that case, there's simply nothing to lose! So for women who are ready to choose a partner and start a family, why not increase the odds by considering younger men?

In the previous several chapters, I discussed a number of benefits that come along with FAYM relationships. The flip side of the equation is the drawbacks that go hand in hand with the traditional, older man/younger woman pairing—like all the baggage that older men have in tow. In the next chapter, I'll tell you what I mean by "baggage and how FAYM relationships help women avoid the extra burden.

CHAPTER 12

"Who Ordered the Older Man with a Side of Baggage?"

In the previous chapter on having babies in a FAYM relationship, I touched on an often-overlooked point: The older a guy is, the more baggage he likely has. Therefore, the question of the older boyfriend's baggage is worthy of its own chapter. What kinds of baggage might a woman inadvertently pick up by dating an older man? What are the odds that she can avoid this extra burden by choosing a FAYM relationship? I'll explore those questions in this chapter; so let's get started.

The most obvious kind of baggage a man might have is, of course, children from a previous marriage. Imagine Rebecca, a 33 year-old woman. She's an attractive, spunky redhead who does PR and marketing for a large art gallery in Denver. In the dating scene, two guys have piqued her interest recently.

First, there's David, a 39 year-old, restaurant owner. He's tall and athletic with a sharp sense of humor. Then, there's Zach, a 28 year-old art teacher. With striking blue eyes, Zach is very well spoken. In addition, a gallery near Rebecca's office just picked his woodcarvings for a small exhibition.

Rebecca sees perks to both relationships. David's restaurant is doing well, so he's often able to treat Rebecca to weekend getaways that she might not necessarily have splurged on for herself. But as the marketing director for a major gallery, Rebecca's making pretty good money, so she's used to an active social life at upscale restaurants, theatres, and concert venues. What's really exciting is that David is connected to several local politicians in Rebecca's party, and he has taken her to fundraising events and benefits where she's had an opportunity to meet these important people and talk about issues important to her. She and David enjoy chatting about current events and reading and hearing about the politicians they've personally met.

But Rebecca loves things about dating Zach too. As a high school teacher, he's not exactly rolling in cash. He does, however, share Rebecca's passion for visual art, and he's able to talk knowledgeably with her about the new artists her gallery displays. He can't treat her to expensive dinners and events like David does, but he's delighted when Rebecca takes him to restaurants he wouldn't be able to try on his own, and he's truly excited to attend her gallery events. In addition, Rebecca found it extremely gratifying, both personally and professionally, when she introduced Zach's woodcarvings to a local gallery curator and secured him an exhibition. Also, she loves spending time with Zach's friends, who make her feel connected to Denver's local artistic community and admire her professional success in their industry.

It sounds like Rebecca's in a good spot, right? She's casually dating two great guys, and when she's ready to start a more serious relationship, she'll be ahead of the curve. But here's the catch: David was married in his late twenties and divorced about two years ago. He has an eight year-old daughter, Lisa, and a six year-old son, Paul. In contrast, Zach has had several serious, long-term girlfriends (one of whom he lived with for a few years), but he's never been married, and he has no children.

David recently invited Rebecca for ice cream with Lisa and Paul. Paul seemed excited to meet Rebecca and was fascinated by her iPhone, but Lisa sat quietly through the whole outing, refusing to talk to Rebecca. She didn't even want any ice cream.

David has always been very up-front with Rebecca about his previous marriage. He explained that the divorce was particularly rough on Lisa, and that while she's a sweet kid, she's having a hard time with the idea of her parents dating new people. David has also been honest with Rebecca about the fact that his joint custody arrangement with Lisa and Paul's mother is somewhat complex. His ex-wife is a journalist who travels often, so David's custody schedule is unpredictable and his first priority. He understandably had to cancel a few dates with Rebecca because he needed to pick up the kids unexpectedly. In addition, he mentioned that his relationship with his ex-wife is somewhat strained. He retains no lingering resentments and has never complained outright to Rebecca, but it's stressful for him to be in constant negotiation with his ex over their children's care, schooling, healthcare, and the endless litany of issues that parenting involves for any couple—married or divorced.

Rebecca is a realistic, grounded person. She has given her relationships with David and with Zach much thought. She likes the fact that David is very forthright with her about his previous marriage and can see that his divorce gives him some perspective on relationships that Zach just doesn't possess. For example, David understands that relationships are real work, and Rebecca trusts that he won't take marital commitment lightly the second time.

On the other hand, Zach is certainly a clear-thinking adult, and he's had enough experience with long-term relationships that Rebecca doesn't feel she has to hold his hand through everything. The fact that he has no children makes things undeniably simpler.

Further, David will continue to have joint-custody and caretaking negotiations on his plate for at least another 12 years—or more, if Lisa and Paul decide to postpone college or starting on their own. Obviously, his role as their father won't end when they come of age. He will always have obligations to them—and eventually to their children. That's not a bad thing, and Rebecca likes kids, especially Lisa and Paul. As a child of divorced parents, Rebecca understands what Lisa is going through and trusts that the two of them would eventually be able to have a warm relationship. Her own childhood experience with her parents' divorce, however, also taught Rebecca that it's an experience that lasts a lifetime—especially when children are involved.

Here's the biggest catch: Lisa and Paul's continued presence in David's life means his ex-wife's continued presence in his life—and eventually, in Rebecca's life if things get more serious with David. Rebecca is sure that David's ex-wife isn't a bad person, but her tense relationship with David would put a strain on Rebecca. Even if things improved over time, the situation would be at best awkward but always inescapable because both David and his ex-wife love their children and want to be present in their lives.

Boiling it all down, David carries all kinds of baggage that Zach doesn't. At the same time, David's baggage is not a trade-off for maturity. He has more money than Zach, sure, and some perspectives on relationships that Zach doesn't yet. But Zach, despite being 11 years younger than David, is just as mature, thoughtful, intelligent, well educated, and willing and able to engage in open communication.

If she chooses Zach, Rebecca would give up hobnobbing with her favorite politicians, but she'd also sidestep a lifetime of divorce-related stresses, tensions, arguments, or just plain awkwardness. Rebecca is ready for the hard work and patience involved in nurturing a lifelong relationship, but she can't help asking herself, "Am I ready for the extra baggage?"

Rebecca starts thinking of her friend Monique. Monique is 37 and has been with her boyfriend Don for four years. In fact, they met when Monique was 33—exactly the age Rebecca is now. Don is six years older than Monique; the same age difference as there is between Rebecca and David.

Like David, Don was divorced when he met Monique and has three young children. Monique and Don are definitely in love; anyone who spends time with them can see it. About two years ago, Monique would tell Rebecca all the time that she was sure a proposal was just around the corner, but the proposal still hasn't come. Don and Rebecca have gotten to be good friends through Monique, and he once admitted to Rebecca that the idea of marrying again worries him. He's scarred by his divorce.

But he loves Monique enormously, and if that were the only issue, he might be willing to take the risk.

But there's a second issue: He also knows how badly Monique wants children. He already has three and just doesn't picture himself having any more, which he and Monique have discussed. Don wonders if it would be fair for him to propose to Monique, knowing that a marriage with him would keep her from having children of her own—one of the things she wants most in life.

In the meantime, Monique confided to Rebecca that she's nervous. She's 37 and knows she doesn't have a tremendous amount of time left to have biological children. Sometimes, she's convinced that Don is the love of her life, but at other times, she wonders if they just met at the wrong place and the wrong time.

She now faces an extremely painful choice: stay with Don and give up having a family of her own or leave Don with whom she has so much fun and so much in common and start looking again—at the age of 37.

Rebecca and Monique are close, and it really hurts Rebecca to see her friend facing such a difficult decision. At the same time, she wonders if she could learn something from seeing Monique deal with this situation. What if Rebecca found herself in the same spot in four years?

Her relationship with David is still too new and casual for the two of them to discuss the possibility of children, but Rebecca definitely wants to start a family, probably in the next couple of years. What if it turns out that David feels he already has all the children he wants? What if Rebecca doesn't realize this is true until she's already in love with him?

On top of those concerns, Rebecca has her mother's advice with which to contend. Rebecca's mother, Anne, divorced at the age of 34 when Rebecca was ten. The divorce was difficult, both emotionally and financially, so it was several years before Anne started dating again in the late 1980s. At that time, she didn't think of dating younger men. It just wasn't something women usually considered. Anne saw several men about eight or ten years older than she was.

Slowly, she noticed a pattern. All of these guys

were born in the early to mid 1940s, and to varying degrees, many of them were unsupportive of Anne's career. Divorced with a teenage daughter preparing to go to college, naturally, she strove for advancements in her career. After her divorce, she attended night school and secured a degree in library sciences. She performed well at her new job but needed to spend extra hours at the library here and there to prove that she was serious and worthy of promotion.

Occasionally, an older guy that Anne dated would be extremely supportive and excited about her career. However, all too often, they either teased her about her cute job as a librarian or acted outright annoyed that her commitment to her career meant she was unwilling to make sacrifices for them.

Anne learned from her experience and pointed out to Rebecca early on that many men born before and during the Women's Movement hadn't truly absorbed the idea of women's equality. She didn't just read my earlier chapter in this book—she lived it. Anne told Rebecca that the younger a man is, the more likely it will be that he grew up in a culture that not only espouses equality but provides young men and women with daily examples. Rebecca took this advice to heart.

Now, as she's faced with choosing between David and Zach, she can't help hearing her mother's voice in her head, "The younger he is, Rebecca, the more likely he'll be to take you seriously as a whole person." At 39, David definitely isn't from the Stone Age. His ex-wife has a successful career, and David never suggested that her working was responsible for their failed marriage. But he certainly emphasizes being the more financially successful and more politically connected partner when they date. That dynamic just doesn't come into play in her interactions with Zach, who values her professional opinion enormously, has just as many female friends as male ones, and grew up with co-ed Power Rangers.

As she makes her choice, Rebecca also thinks of another friend, Katie.

Katie, who is also 33, prefers to date men a little older than she is. She thinks dating younger guys is "kinda weird"—though she can't really say why. She's succumbed to cultural pressures. She always pushes Rebecca to "go for" David, whom she considers the right man because he's older. But the stories she tells Rebecca about her own dating misadventures are harrowing.

Katie has been on a string of dates with guys in their mid to late thirties who are clearly just serial daters with no thought of commitment. Or worse, the guys she goes out with are so embittered from hurt, rejection, and disappointment that they carry enormous chips on their shoulders—yet another form of baggage with dating older people. At best,

Katie can tell they're spending the whole date thinking, "Well, this one won't work out either." At worst, they've concluded that their disappointments are all the women's fault.

In fact, Katie has spent a few first dates with men who complained about their previous girlfriends and actually said things like "women are only after a guy's money." Rebecca definitely sympathizes with Katie as she's been out with a few of these guys, too. But she can't help thinking, "This wouldn't be a problem if Katie would just consider younger guys."

When Rebecca looks at all the pros and cons this way, her choice is clear. It's not that Zach is a better man than David; Rebecca likes and respects both of them. But she knows full well from witnessing her parents' breakup and what seems like an outright divorce plague among her friends and coworkers that maintaining a serious and loving relationship is no small commitment.

Our society already puts a lot of pressure on couples from finances to childrearing. Why add more uncontrollable factors to the equation? Although she has had fun with David, Rebecca ultimately decides that there will simply be too many stresses on their relationship. By choosing Zach, she can just focus on falling in love—not on outside forces that would detract from the relationship.

I can attest to the validity of Rebecca's concerns

because I've been through a lot of them myself. Like Rebecca's friend Katie, I went on every kind of date imaginable when I was single. I dated until I was 40, and in that time, I dated divorced men with small children, guys who had been single all their lives and were pushing 45, and guys who were pushing 45, had been married, and divorced three times. I dated every type.

I also discovered that older single guys tend to go in one of two directions: Either they're completely jaded by their years of unsuccessful dating, or they're so used to bachelorhood and playing the field that they wouldn't settle down for anything. In fact, I once had a guy invite me on a date to a singles event! When he realized his faux pas, he apologized and explained that he had just gotten so used to going to singles events he didn't know what else to do.

It's almost an epidemic among singles—both men and women—once they've been on the scene for years without any success, they develop a bad attitude toward dating. It's possible to sidestep that attitude entirely by choosing partners who are a little "newer" to the game and haven't yet had time to get "tired of dating new people."

Rebecca's experience with David's daughter Lisa is another to which I can relate. I ultimately chose to marry a man slightly older than I am. (After all, that's what this book is about: You fall in love with whomever you happen to fall in love with, and there's no reason to put arbitrary age restrictions—in either direction—on your relationships!) In the beginning, my husband's son didn't even want to meet me. Now, ten years later, we developed a wonderful friendship. However, it took time and effort on both our parts. Before we arrived at this point, I experienced the pain of being a woman in love with a man whose child didn't like me. I knew how important my husband's children were to him, and it hurt all of us. I know it was hard on my stepson and my stepdaughter to see their father with a "stranger."

As I discovered with my husband, every relationship has its particular difficulties, and each person has to decide for himself or herself when the power of the relationship is worth overcoming specific hardships. For me, the "baggage" of a previous marriage was something I ultimately decided I was willing to pick up because I had indeed found my soul mate. Luckily, his children were also willing to get to know me and to work with me in creating a new relationship.

The reality is that any amount of baggage doesn't automatically mean that love is impossible or doomed, but it's time for women to realize that baggage isn't an inevitable part of dating after 30. This dynamic can very often be sidestepped entirely by choosing a FAYM relationship. Thus, "avoiding his baggage" is just one more bullet point to add to our growing list of perks for FAYM relationships.

I've made it clear over the course of this book that FAYM relationships involve balanced, mutual relationships between people with a relatively small age gap—up to about ten years. However, when most people think of a "younger partner," whether male or female, the image that pops up is of the "trophy wife" or "pool boy boyfriend."

Our culture is fascinated by the idea of a wealthy and powerful person who can attract a much younger, sexy plaything. That's definitely not what FAYM relationships are about, but it's a fascinating phenomenon to explore.

In the next chapter, I'll investigate that juicy side note. What happens when women date not just younger men, but *much* younger men?

CHAPTER 13

The Trophy Boyfriend

My friend—we'll call her Sarah—divorced when she was fairly young. In the divorce settlement, she received custody of her two young children as well as half of a very small neighborhood business that she and her ex-husband had founded. In the years and even decades after the divorce, Sarah worked tirelessly. She barely took any time for herself, and as far as anyone could tell, she didn't date at all. Instead, she raised her children and, at the same time, built her half of the business into what is now a major, multimillion-dollar corporation.

Then, many years after her divorce, after her children were grown, she went on vacation and met a handsome, charming man who happened to pique her interest in a way that no one else had for all that time. He also happened to be younger than she was— by about 25 years.

The two of them have been together for ten years. They live in her fantastic home; she shares her lifestyle with him from grocery shopping together to attending all the upscale events that come with running a major corporation. All her friends and family know him and expect to see them together. After so many years of working hard and raising her children, Sarah rewarded herself with a partner who is full of life, ready to help her enjoy the fruits of her labor, and quite a bit younger than she is. Other than the age difference, they seem to be a traditional couple, holding hands and very attentive to one another. They look happy together.

I'll be honest: I doubt Sarah's experience with her much younger beau is the norm. More often, when we see a couple with a huge age gap (where typically the younger partner is female), we think, "Yikes. That's not love, that's a financial arrangement." That's why, throughout this book, I've stressed that FAYM relationships are not about a large age gap. I've defined FAYM relationships as being between a woman and a man up to ten years younger than she is. Larger age gaps start to represent significant percentages of a person's life, and that's when we stray into the territory of a power imbalance in the relationship.

However, this situation happens visibly in America today: A few women are starting to choose much younger partners. It is just a few, however, enough women have done so that it has become noticeable. So what's going on? This kind of relationship pushes the extreme of the FAYM model, but it's worth exploring as a kind of interesting side note to the rest of this book.

In the past, when people talked about couples with huge age gaps, the image automatically coming to mind was the rich but graying man with a buxom blonde on his arm, the sugar daddy with his trophy wife or girlfriend. Certainly, older men with much younger women still make up the vast majority of relationships with a large age difference. But more and more, we start to see a new kind of couple out on the town: the trophy boyfriend.

It's not a huge trend, by any means, and it's certainly not happening with the same frequency as FAYM relationships.

In fact, the *New York Times Magazine* recently did

a story called "Keeping Up with Being Kept" about the latest trend in "sugar daddy dating." The article tells the tale of a new—and surprisingly successful—website called SeekingArrangement.com. It's a dating site geared toward pairing wealthy but "more mature" adults with young partners. Right there on their profiles, "sugar babies" can advertise the sum of the "allowance" they're looking for, and "sugar daddies and sugar mommies" can advertise their net worth.

Here's the interesting thing: According to this article, "sugar mommies" only make up about 1 percent of the site's membership. If that's any evidence, it's possible to say that the overwhelming majority of the time, relationships with huge age gaps happen between older men and younger women. But enough women are in the market for a much younger man that the site has found it necessary to accommodate them. I doubt that would have been true ten years ago.

The trophy boyfriend trend, in a way, logically extends from the FAYM relationship trend. Women have discovered by the thousands that there is no longer any economical, biological, cultural, or any other reason they can't date a man a couple years younger— just as men have been doing with younger women since the beginning of time.

The same economic factors that make it possible for women to date slightly younger men now make

it possible for women to date *a lot* younger men. Not only do women work today, but they do so at high-power, high-stress, and high-yield jobs as CEOs, CFOs, doctors, lawyers, and hedge fund managers; you name it, and women do it. Women now have the financial power to attract youth and good looks.

Not only is it now possible for women to be financially independent, but it's also culturally acceptable for women to stray from the old model of family. Women today don't necessarily look for a man to take care of them, and they aren't automatically expected to want to bear and raise children. Consequently, it's perfectly possible for a single, middle-age woman to seek companionship without the goal of starting a family. Either she's never had children and doesn't want them, or her children are grown, and she's not interested in having more.

If this is her situation, it's not unreasonable for her to think, "Why not choose a much younger man?" The goal isn't to form the bedrock of a family but rather to have fun and enjoy each other's company. In Sarah's case, she deserves to think about herself after all these years, and reward herself with some fun and a handsome companion.

Granted, just because FAYM relationships are gaining cultural acceptance doesn't necessarily mean trophy boyfriend relationships are going to become equally acceptable. Even before trophy boyfriends became a possibility for increasing numbers of women, society never exactly applauded their original incarnation: the trophy girlfriend arrangement.

A man's buddies and colleagues might be kind of impressed—or even a little envious—when he shows up with a 25 year-old bombshell on his arm, but for the most part, everyone understands the exchange involved in these kinds of relationships, and it doesn't fit our culture's idealized conception of love and partnership. This thin, vivacious young woman probably does not look at her boyfriend through rose-colored glasses. She knows that his hair is gray, his eyebrows bushy, his skin loose and flecked with age spots, and his belly expanding. But she has decided—for better or for worse—that she's willing to trade in looks for charisma, charm, worldly opinions, connections to important people, tickets to hot events, travel . . . and, yes, a full wallet.

For example, would any woman describe Bill Gates as a real looker? He's not a decrepit old man, but he's the consummate geek. If he were single, though, women would probably line up around the block to date him. He's incredibly smart, and he—by all evidence—has a superhumanly generous spirit. He gives the majority of his money away to his foundation.

So here you have one of the smartest, kindest men in the world also happens to be one of the wealthiest men in the world. Many women would willingly overlook the thick, square glasses and Beatles mop for a chance to date him. Likely, they would notice his less-than-ideal looks, but they'd be eager to make the trade. For all I know, he's that "nice man with a good sense of humor" women all say they're seeking. Still, his wealth must make him more appealing than he would be otherwise.

For the first time ever, people are discovering that despite mean-spirited generalizations about "gold diggers," it's not just sexy young women who are willing to make the trade-off of looks and youth for money and connections. Plenty of sexy young men would make the trade if given the chance. Now, they have the opportunity to do so for pretty much the first time in American history. Maybe in the past, a few rich heiresses or widows kept a younger boyfriend, but for the most part, the trophy boyfriend hasn't been an economic possibility for women until today.

Similarly, men aren't the only ones inclined to reward themselves for their success by "acquiring" a much younger companion. Women who have earned money and power might also enjoy the ego boost of having a boy toy. These kinds of "special arrangements" are not necessarily our society's conception of an ideal pairing, and they're not what I've been advocating over the course of this book. It seems clear that a few of them develop into warm, loving, mutual relationships as in the case of my friend Sarah.

However, these relationships might be a sort of necessary step in the infancy of the FAYM relationship trend. When society discovers a new freedom, there's a tendency to take it to its extreme. As previously discussed, it's a bit like the explosion of sexual freedom that happened immediately after the widespread release of the birth control pill. For a few years afterwards, many women went wild, knowing that pregnancy was no longer an uncontrollable consequence of sex. However, after a few years of total liberty, people calmed down again. Most of them just used the birth control pill as a part of their plain old monogamous sex lives.

We're likely to see the same kind of curve in the trend of women seeking trophy boyfriends. As the FAYM relationship trend gains acceptance, many women may experiment with taking it to the edge. We'll probably see this offshoot of the trend peak fairly soon, and it won't necessarily last as a major cultural phenomenon. A few women will always choose this kind of relationship, but for the most part, we're not going to see it as the norm—just as it's not the norm for men to have very young trophy girlfriends.

I would guess that when no fault divorce first began to be an option in many states, there was a huge spike in men having midlife crises at 47 and suddenly deciding they needed a new red convertible and a 20 year-old girlfriend. But now, while a few men decide they need a new car and a new girl, most of them make it through their fiftieth birthdays by buying a set of new golf clubs, adding Grecian Formula to their grooming regimen, and going on a dream vacation with their wives.

The same thing will happen with the trophy boyfriend trend. This isn't the new picture of love in America; it's just one option that will work for a small minority of women. Now, as is the case with my friend Sarah, trophy boyfriend relationships are not always just a financial arrangement.

It's entirely possible that there's a lot of mutual respect, care, and even love between a woman and a much younger boyfriend. As with men and their much younger girlfriends, the more mature partner often takes on the role of mentor and provides guidance and financial support for their younger sweetheart's personal and professional goals. That often turns into a solid foundation for a loving relationship. It's easy to love someone generous with his or her care, concern, attention, and money. Sometimes, these relationships do develop into lasting partnerships that trump the odds and skepticism of society.

Nevertheless, a little realism is still needed. In reality, despite all the Cosmopolitan magazine covers we've seen, not every woman looks like a supermodel (and not every man looks like David Beckham, for that matter). Once you get past the eye candy in the celebrity magazines and websites and start dealing with the real world, physical attraction is only one part of the reason why people get—and stay—married. In the real world, attraction certainly plays a role, but it's hardly the only connection point between men and women. It's also about shared values, religious sensibilities, and a host of other topics, which have nothing to do with looks.

Indeed, in a typical FAYM relationship, the 53 year-old woman usually doesn't look any older than her 49 year-old boyfriend does. But if she wants a great-looking, 29 year-old boyfriend . . . that's a different story. She either has to look like Madonna or her bank statement has to look like Madonna's – or both.

In sum, whether you're looking for a trophy boyfriend, a happily-ever-after relationship, or something in between, if you're open to the FAYM concept (as a man or as a woman), you're part of a big new trend and you've increased your chances of finding love by 100 percent.

www.ingramcontent.com/pod-product-compliance
Lightning Source LLC
Chambersburg PA
CBHW070801240726

48654CB00007B/172